Traveling Light:
New Paths for
International Tourism

LISA MASTNY

Jane A. Peterson, *Editor*

WORLDWATCH PAPER 159

December 2001

FINANCIAL SUPPORT for the Institute is provided by the Geraldine R. Dodge Foundation, the Ford Foundation, the Richard & Rhoda Goldman Fund, the William and Flora Hewlett Foundation, W. Alton Jones Foundation, Charles Stewart Mott Foundation, the Curtis and Edith Munson Foundation, David and Lucile Packard Foundation, John D. and Catherine T. MacArthur Foundation, Summit Foundation, Surdna Foundation, Inc., Turner Foundation, Inc., U.N. Environment Programme, U.N. Population Fund, Wallace Genetic Foundation, Wallace Global Fund, Weeden Foundation, and the Winslow Foundation. The Institute also receives financial support from its Council of Sponsors members—Tom and Cathy Crain, James and Deanna Dehlsen, Roger and Vicki Sant, Robert Wallace and Raisa Scriabine, and Eckart Wintzen—and from the many other friends of Worldwatch.

Table of Contents

Figures and Tables

ACKNOWLEDGMENTS: Many thanks to Bas Amelung, Robyn Bushell, Frans de Man, Megan Epler Wood, Anita Pleumarom, Geoff Wall, and Pam Wight for their thoughtful comments on earlier drafts of this paper. Thanks also to Jayakumar Chelaton, Attilio Costaguta, Stefan Gössling, Rosa Songel, Sheryl Spivack, Neil Tangri, and Mark Woodward for their valuable insights and kind help with data and information.

At Worldwatch, editor Jane Peterson strengthened the concept of the paper, while Linda Starke helped with tightening. Hilary French served as a research mentor, and Gary Gardner offered much-needed moral support. Uta Saoshiro persistently tracked down elusive facts, while Janet Abramovitz, Erik Assadourian, Seth Dunn, Brian Halweil, Anne Platt McGinn, Danielle Nierenberg, and Michael Renner provided helpful comments on an earlier draft. Liz Doherty transformed the text and figures into a work of art, while Dick Bell, Leanne Mitchell, and Niki Clark helped to hone and communicate the message. And Payal Sampat and Denise Warden carefully proofread the final draft.

Finally, heartfelt thanks to my parents, Catherine Mastny-Fox and Vojtech Mastny, for providing solid intellectual leadership, and to John Lamoreux for his patience, rationality, and constant support.

LISA MASTNY is a staff researcher at the Worldwatch Institute, where she studies a wide range of economics and development topics. She is a contributing author of the Institute's annual books, *State of the World* and *Vital Signs*. And she has written for *World Watch* magazine on ecotourism, global ice melting, and environmental and social change in the Arctic. Before joining Worldwatch in 1998, she worked briefly at the U.S. Environmental Protection Agency, at Germany's Wuppertal Institute, and at a cultural tourism group in the Czech Republic. Lisa holds Master's degrees in International Relations and Environmental Studies from Yale University and a Bachelor's degree in International Studies from Johns Hopkins University.

Introduction

When Kovalam, a small fishing village in India's Kerala state, began to lose its tourist trade after 20 boom years, residents were at first baffled. Why had the stream of visitors eager to enjoy its palm-lined beaches slowed to a trickle? By 2000, hotels, restaurants, and souvenir shops were scrambling for dwindling tourist dollars.[1]

At first, experts and tour operators wondered if economic factors and shifting tourist tastes accounted for the drying up of tourism, but there was no evidence of either. Finally, they discovered the culprit: mushrooming piles of garbage had tainted the reputation of the village. Like many destinations in the developing world, Kovalam has no official plan to deal with waste management. While hotels and other facilities collect recyclable items for reuse by local industries whenever possible, the more stubborn refuse—human waste, plastic bottles, and other non-biodegradables—simply accumulates in towering mounds or is dumped outside the village center.[2]

Jayakumar Chelaton, a local activist, attributes recent outbreaks of cholera and other diseases to the deteriorating water quality and sanitation conditions. But "nobody bothers about the health issues faced by the locals," he explains. "Everybody wants Kovalam beach to be clean so it can get more business." The options have generally been limited: a proposal for an incinerator was shelved after local residents and environmental groups objected, and all short-term plans have involved simply dumping the waste elsewhere.[3]

Across the developing world, communities are trying to come to terms with the mixed impacts of booming tourism, one of the largest and fastest-growing sectors of the global economy. Directly and indirectly, travel and tourism activities accounted for some $3.6 trillion of economic activity in 2000—or roughly 11 percent of the gross world product. Since 1950, the number of international tourist arrivals has increased nearly 28-fold, to some 698 million. These figures are expected to again double by 2020, to an estimated 1.6 billion arrivals. Although fears concerning terrorism and the safety of air travel have dampened tourism demand for the time being, over the long term this activity is expected to resume its rapid growth.[4]

As the rules of the global economy change, and as tourist desires shift, destinations like Europe and North America are becoming less dominant in the international tourism market. Meanwhile, visits to Asia, Africa, and elsewhere in the developing world have increased dramatically in the last 25 years. One in every five international tourists now travels from an industrial country to a developing one, up from one in 13 in the mid-1970s.[5]

Rushing to capitalize on their rich natural and cultural attractions, many developing countries welcome tourism as a way to stimulate investments, generate foreign exchange earnings, and diversify their economies. Tourism can be more lucrative and less resource-intensive than growing a single cash crop or pursuing traditional industries like mining, oil development, and manufacturing.[6]

These tourism investments appear to be paying off. Tourism is the only sector where developing countries consistently run a trade surplus. It represents roughly 10 percent of developing-world exports and accounts for more than 40 percent of the gross domestic product in some countries. An estimated 65 percent of the roughly 200 million jobs created by tourism annually are found in the developing world.[7]

Because it provides so many jobs, tourism can be a powerful vehicle to boost the income of many the world's people—including traditionally disadvantaged groups such as women. Yet governments and tourism businesses have largely overlooked opportunities to harness tourism's development potential and to spread its benefits more widely. Instead, tourism remains one of the world's least regulated industries, a situation that often has negative implications for local economies, cultures, and ecosystems.[8]

Without significant efforts to divert tourism from its current path, important ground may even be lost. Spurred by a rapidly changing and increasingly centralized global economy, many governments are under pressure to grant outside investors—such as international hotel chains and tour operations—easier access to tourism assets. The influx of these businesses threatens to crowd out the smaller, homegrown tourism enterprises that form the backbone of the tourism industry. Already, as much as half of the tourism revenue that enters the developing world "leaks" back out—through profits earned by foreign-owned businesses, promotional spending abroad, or to pay for imported labor and goods.[9]

Tourism also has uneven impacts on indigenous cultures. On the one hand, it can bring greater revenue and respect to minority groups, helping to meet basic needs and to sustain or revive languages, religious traditions, and other practices that might otherwise be lost. But many indigenous communities end up as passive participants in ventures that are promoted and run from the outside, leaving them little say in the changes that tourism brings.[10]

As in India's Kovalam, tourism is also causing serious environmental damage in the developing world. The sheer numbers of tourists, as well as the facilities built to accommodate them, are straining ecosystems at many destinations. Tourist transport, hotels, golf courses, and other developments typically require huge amounts of energy, water, and other resources, often at the expense of local users. They also generate considerable waste and pollution in destinations that are not prepared to deal with these impacts.[11]

To address some of these problems, many countries are embracing ecotourism—a more responsible form of travel that generates money and jobs while also seeking to protect local environments and cultures. But even though it does succeed in some circumstances, ecotourism is not always the answer. For one thing, not every place is suited to this type of tourism. And when done poorly, ecotourism suffers from many of the same environmental and social pitfalls as conventional tourism—including using resources irresponsibly, creating waste, and endangering ecosystems. In some cases, it has become little more than a green marketing tool used by enterprises hoping to promote an image of environmental consciousness.[12]

As the impacts of tourism continue to spread, it is increasingly important to steer it onto a more sustainable path—economically, culturally, and environmentally. This will require deep sectoral changes that reach far beyond the scope of ecotourism. A broad range of stakeholders—including the tourism industry, governments, international organizations, nongovernmental groups (NGOs), host communities, and tourists themselves—will need to be involved in sustainability efforts at all levels.

Fortunately, many of these groups are already moving forward on some of the key issues. For instance, while concerns about tourism merely hovered at the fringes of discussions at the 1992 U.N. Conference on Environment and Development in Rio de Janeiro, they have moved to the center of preparations for the follow-up World Summit on Sustainable Development in September 2002.

Many hotels, tour operators, and other tourism businesses are already taking steps to incorporate environmental and social sustainability measures into their daily operations, including reducing resource use and improving the treatment and handling of waste. Companies are also embracing a wide range of voluntary initiatives, from developing environmental and social codes of conduct for their staff and clients to working to meet benchmarks for a diversity of tourism certification efforts.

Yet industry action alone is not enough to ensure sustainable tourism development. Governments at the national, regional, and local levels can supplement industry initiatives by implementing a wide range of policies and regulatory measures, from restricting environmentally damaging construction to limiting the number of visitors allowed at sensitive sites. And they can work with citizens' groups and other NGOs to help local communities take charge of their own futures, providing them with the training and resources they need to oversee and manage local tourism developments.

Meanwhile, tourists themselves can play a valuable role in steering tourism onto new paths. Visitor education programs can help tourists become more aware of the impacts of their own activities on local ecosystems, economies, and cultures, and spur important changes in travel choice and behavior.

Ultimately, no form of tourism will be truly sustainable, as any activity that encourages large numbers of people to visit remote or fragile sites will inevitably put pressure on resources and communities. The most sustainable option of all would be to stay at home. But in a world where travel is an increasingly important vehicle for cultural exchange, as well as a crucial driver of the global economy, this is an impractical and unrealistic solution. People will always want to explore the planet's diversity; the challenge is to ensure that the travel experiences of the future will be as rewarding as those today.[13]

A Global Industry

Travel has long been a part of the human experience. Early voyagers set out to colonize new territories, wage war, go on pilgrimage, or, like 13th century Italian explorer Marco Polo, to establish new trade routes across unfamiliar continents. Some wanderers were involuntary refugees who had little choice but to move from place to place, spurred on by famine, disease, or political or religious persecution. Often, they faced hostile and dangerous conditions, with constant threats from bandits, bad weather, wild animals, and diseases like plague and cholera.[14]

With the advent of the Industrial Revolution in the late 18th century, travel became easier, at least for more privileged segments of society. Sturdier roads, railways, and steam-powered transport shortened journey times, and industrial expansion generated greater wealth, giving birth to new concepts like leisure and paid vacation. Aristocrats embarked on extended visits to health spas, and on their "Grand Tours" of continental Europe.[15]

The rise of the Romantic Age around 1800 sparked a new desire to seek out the unknown. Writers and artists were drawn to foreign regions by the mystique of exotic scenery, mountains, and cultures, and anthropologists and biologists launched expeditions in search of remote lands and peoples. By the end of the 19th century, an entire tourism industry had emerged to accommodate the enterprising traveler, complete with booking agents, guidebooks, package tours, hotels, railways, and organized timetables.[16]

Over the next century, the popularization of the automobile and the expansion of roads and highways accelerated the pace of cross-continental travel, particularly in Europe and North America. But it was only after World War II, with the emergence of wide-bodied commercial jets, cheap oil, and low promotional airfares, that international tourism became accessible to broader segments of the global population.[17]

The World Tourism Organization, a United Nations-affiliated research and support group based in Madrid, collects data on the global reach of tourism, and helps its 133 member countries strengthen and promote their tourism sectors. It defines tourism as the activities of people who travel "outside their usual environment" for more than a year for leisure, business, and other purposes. According to the organization, the number of international tourists has increased nearly 28-fold since 1950, reaching

FIGURE 1

International Tourist Arrivals, 1950–2000

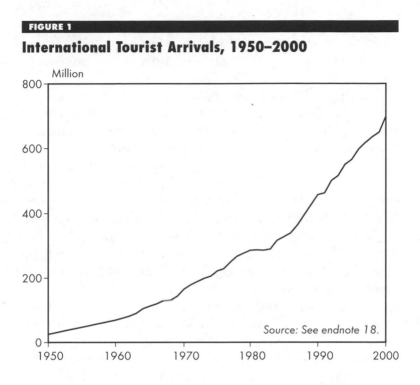

Source: See endnote 18.

698 million arrivals in 2000. (See Figure 1.) These numbers are expected to again double by 2020, to 1.6 billion, although all estimates cited in this paper were made before the September 2001 terrorism attacks in the United States. The numbers also leave out the millions of people who travel domestically—the vast majority of the world's tourists, and a figure that would make estimates between four and 10 times higher, depending on the location.[18]

Significant advances in travel technology have accelerated tourism's growth. New global distribution systems and computer reservation systems enable agents to check flight availability, issue tickets, and make airline, hotel, and car rental reservations rapidly. And increasingly, individual travelers—mostly in industrial countries—access this information directly over the Internet, often at significantly lower cost. The Travel Industry Association of America reports that the number of on-line bookings of flights and other travel-related services increased fivefold between 1997 and 2000, to 25 million. Consumers spent more than $13 billion on these services in 2000, compared with only $800 million in 1997.[19]

Despite the numbers, tourism remains restricted to a tiny, more affluent share of the world's population. Nearly 80 percent of international tourists come from Europe and the Americas, while only 15 percent originate in East Asia and the Pacific and 5 percent in Africa, the Middle East, and South Asia combined. Yet even these figures are deceptive: in the United States, a leading source of tourists worldwide, fewer than a fifth of citizens hold valid passports. All told, just 3.5 percent of the world's population travels internationally. This share is expected to double to 7 percent by 2020, assuming a continuing rise in global prosperity and a decline in the cost of travel.[20]

Today, nearly two thirds of international tourists travel for vacation, leisure, and recreation, as opposed to visiting friends and relatives or traveling for health, business, and religious purposes. But tourist tastes are gradually changing. According to researcher Auliana Poon, growing displeasure with heavily commercialized, overrun, and polluted destinations is spurring a shift from the highly packaged and standardized mass tourism of the past half-century. In its place, rising numbers of more flexible and independent travelers are pursuing more personalized experiences like exploring culture or nature. A study of U.S. travelers in the early 1990s supported this shift: while 20 percent of respondents were "after the sun," 40 percent sought more "life-enhancing" travel.[21]

These changes in travel preferences are reflected in surveys of the most popular destinations worldwide. Although Europe and the Americas continue to attract the most international tourists (the majority from within these regions themselves), they no longer draw the same proportion of visitors as in 1950. (See Figure 2.) Meanwhile, tourism to and within Asia, the Middle East, Africa, and South Asia is growing rapidly.[22]

FIGURE 2

Share of International Tourist Arrivals by Region, 1950 and 2000, with Projections for 2020

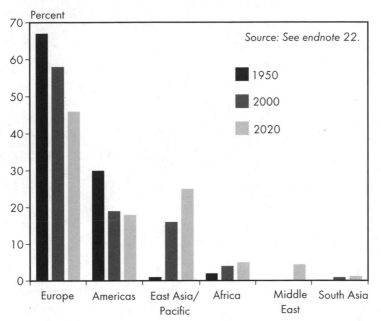

The share of international tourists traveling to East Asia and the Pacific rose from just 1 percent in 1950 to 16 percent in 2000. The World Tourism Organization attributes this increase to rapid population growth, heavy marketing, and growing prosperity in the region. It predicts that by 2020 Asia will be the most popular destination after Europe, attracting more than a quarter of world tourist traffic. China is expected to unseat France as the world's most visited country, and to become the fourth largest *source* of tourists worldwide—behind Germany, Japan, and the United States. (See Table 1.) Russia and former Eastern bloc countries also rank among the top destinations of the future.[23]

As it spreads geographically, tourism is assuming a greater role on the world economic stage, but the complex nature of tourism activities makes measuring this contribution difficult. The World Tourism Organization estimates

TABLE 1

Top 10 Tourist Destinations and Share of Arrivals, 2000, and Projections for 2020

2000		2020	
Destination	Share of Arrivals (percent)	Destination	Share of Arrivals (percent)
France	11.0	China[1]	8.6
United States	7.3	United States	6.4
Spain	6.9	France	5.8
Italy	5.9	Spain	4.4
China[1]	4.5	Hong Kong	3.7
United Kingdom	3.6	Italy	3.3
Russia	3.0	United Kingdom	3.3
Mexico	3.0	Mexico	3.1
Canada	2.9	Russia	2.9
Germany	2.7	Czech Republic	2.7
Top 10 Total	50.6	Top 10 Total	44.2

[1]Excluding Hong Kong
Source: See endnote 23.

that between 1975 and 2000, international tourism receipts—the revenue generated from tourist spending abroad on such items as lodging, food, entertainment, tours, and in-country transport—grew 35 percent faster than the world economy as a whole. They surged from only $13 billion in 1950 to $469 billion in 2000 (in 1999 dollars), and are expected to quadruple over the next two decades, reaching more than $2 trillion. (See Figure 3.) These numbers would be an estimated 18 percent higher if they included international airfares, and four times higher if they included domestic tourism spending.[24]

In terms of gross earnings, industrial countries remain the undisputed economic heavyweights of tourism. Europe, not surprisingly, is the top earner of tourism receipts worldwide, followed by the Americas and Asia. Countries in Europe and North America dominate the lists of tourism's top 10 spenders and earners; China is the only developing

FIGURE 3

International Tourism Receipts, 1950–2000

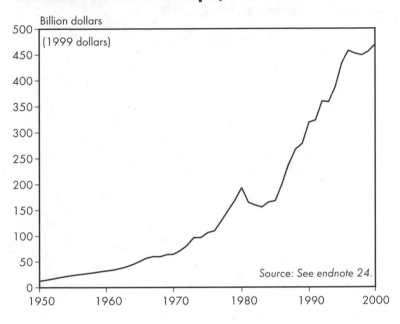

Billion dollars

(1999 dollars)

Source: See endnote 24.

country on either list. (See Table 2.)[25]

Tourism represents a rapidly rising share of world trade. Any tourism service that a visitor buys when traveling abroad is considered an export from the country being visited. In 1999, international tourist spending abroad accounted for nearly 8 percent of world exports of goods and services, surpassing trade in such items as food, textiles, and chemicals. Tourism is also the most rapidly growing export in the services sector, representing more than 40 percent of services exports worldwide. And its predominance in trade is widespread: according to the World Tourism Organization, it ranks among the top five export categories for 83 percent of countries, and is the leading source of foreign exchange earnings for at least 38 percent of them.[26]

Another way to measure the economic impact of tourism is to look at its wider effects throughout a country. In addition to boosting revenue to hotels, restaurants, travel

TABLE 2

Top 10 Spenders and Earners of International Tourism Receipts and Share of Total, 2000

Spenders	Share of Total	Earners	Share of Total
	(percent)		(percent)
United States	14.0	United States	18.0
Germany	10.0	Spain	6.5
United Kingdom	7.7	France	6.3
Japan	6.6	Italy	5.8
France	3.6	United Kingdom	4.1
Italy	3.2	Germany	3.7
Canada	2.6	China	3.4
Netherlands	2.5	Austria	2.4
China	n.a.	Canada	2.3
Belgium/Luxembourg	n.a.	Greece	1.9
Top 10 Total	50.2	Top 10 Total	54.4

Source: See endnote 25.

agencies, tour operators, and transport services, tourism stimulates expansion in other economic sectors like agriculture and construction, creating new markets and generating jobs and income. Measuring this wider reach, the World Travel & Tourism Council, a London-based industry group, estimates that travel and tourism accounted for some $3.6 trillion of economic activity in 2000—or roughly 11 percent of gross world product, making it the world's largest industry. Directly and indirectly, tourism activities also supported an estimated 200 million jobs in 2000, representing 8 percent of total world employment—one in every 12 jobs.[27]

Today, as much as 90 percent of the world's tourism enterprises are small or medium-sized businesses, from one-person snorkeling operations to family-owned inns. But like other sectors in today's global economy, tourism is becoming increasingly consolidated. Between 1997 and 1999, mergers and acquisitions in the hotel and restaurant sector alone exceeded $19 billion, more than in the previous seven years combined. In 1998, the world's 10 leading airlines earned an estimated two thirds of the profits of the roughly 270 airlines that belong to the International Air Transport Association. And in 1999, the top five hotel chains—among them Marriott International, Bass Hotels and Resorts, and Choice Hotels International—managed roughly 14 percent of the world's hotel rooms. Meanwhile, four European tour operators alone handled trips for some 50 million tourists in 2000.[28]

A driving factor behind this consolidation is the unregulated nature of the tourism industry compared with other service sectors. It is increasingly easy for international businesses interested in tourism to enter markets worldwide. This is especially true as more governments privatize national airlines and other state services, reduce domestic subsidies, embrace market reforms, and liberalize trade and investment policies more generally.[29]

Many developing countries, in particular, are opening their markets to tourism in an effort to improve their chances on the world economic stage. But whether this actually brings widespread benefits will depend on the extent to which governments and the industry balance the drive for more tourists with the need for more socially and culturally responsible tourism development.

A Force for Development?

From Asia to the Caribbean, the developing world has experienced a phenomenal surge in tourism in recent years. The number of international tourists now traveling from an industrial country to a developing one increased from only one in 13 in the mid-1970s to one in five in the late 1990s. Destinations like Cambodia, Egypt, Thailand, Turkey, and Viet Nam are rapidly becoming popular. In the Caribbean, arrivals to Cuba have risen more than fivefold since 1990. Overall, tourism growth rates in the developing world are expected to exceed 5 percent a year through 2020, outpacing both the world average and anticipated growth in industrial countries. (Again, the effect of the September 2001 terrorism events on these long-term projections is not yet clear.)[30]

Across the developing world, governments have poured money into tourism marketing, infrastructure projects like roads and hotels, and both large and small tourism businesses. To stimulate tourism investments, many countries offer promotional assistance as well as economic incentives like tax and import duty exemptions, subsidies, and guarantees. By luring tourist dollars, they hope to diversify their economies and attract the foreign exchange needed to reduce heavy debt burdens, pay for imports, strengthen domestic infrastructure, and boost social services like education and health care.[31]

Multilateral lending institutions like the World Bank and the International Monetary Fund (IMF) are behind many of these efforts. After disbanding its tourism department in the mid-1980s, the World Bank renewed its interest in the sector in 1998 and now supports investments in tourism infrastructure and training, site development, and heritage as part of a new institutional focus on poverty alleviation and cultural preservation. In 2000, the International Finance Corporation (IFC), a World Bank agency that makes loans directly to the private sector, supported some $500 million of tourism-related projects, mostly urban revitalization and hotel rehabilitation projects. The IMF, meanwhile, promotes tourism as an export strategy under its economic structural adjustment policies. Many regional lending banks are also involved in tourism-related projects.[32]

In gross economic terms, these investments are beginning to pay off. In a survey of the world's 100 poorest countries done for the U.K. Department for International Development, researchers found that tourism is "significant"—that is, it accounts for at least 2 percent of the gross domestic product (GDP) or 5 percent of exports—in nearly half of the nations in the lowest income range and almost all

TABLE 3

International Tourism Receipts as a Share of GDP in Selected Countries, 1999

Country	Tourism Receipts	Share of GDP
	(million dollars)	(percent)
Maldives	325	88
St. Lucia	311	48
Antigua and Barbuda	291	45
Macao	2,466	40
Barbados	677	27
Vanuatu	56	23
Seychelles	112	21
Jamaica	1,279	19
Belize	112	15
Costa Rica	1,002	7
Egypt	3,903	4
Nepal	168	3
Kenya	304	3
Italy	28,359	2
France	31,507	2
South Africa	2,526	2
China	14,098	1
Rwanda	17	1
United States	74,881	1
Brazil	3,994	1

Source: See endnote 33.

in the lower-to-middle income range. The study also found that tourism is significant or growing in all but one of the 12 countries that are home to 80 percent of the world's poor—including Brazil, China, Indonesia, Nepal, Peru, and the Philippines. Many countries rely heavily on tourism: in some small island nations in the Caribbean and Pacific, it brings in more than 40 percent of GDP. (See Table 3.)[33]

For the world's 49 so-called least developed countries, most of which are in Africa or Asia, tourism is one of few ways to actually participate in the global economy. The U.N. Conference on Trade and Development (UNCTAD) reports that tourism is now the second largest source of foreign exchange after oil in these countries, accounting for 16 percent of total non-oil receipts in 1998. Their aggregate tourism revenue more than doubled between 1992 and 1998, to $2.2 billion, with five countries—Cambodia, Maldives, Nepal, Tanzania, and Uganda—attracting more than half of this 1998 total.[34]

The World Trade Organization reports that tourism is the only economic sector where developing countries consistently run a trade surplus. And its importance in trade is growing. In 1999, international tourism receipts accounted for two thirds of services exports in these countries and more than 10 percent of total exports. (In industrial countries, meanwhile, tourism represented only about one third of services exports and 7 percent of total exports.)[35]

Despite the potential benefits, however, some countries still invest very little in tourism. They may lack the political commitment to develop adequate tourism policies, or they may be forced to devote such a large share of their GDP to servicing foreign debts and meeting other export requirements that they cannot afford to invest in the lodging, food, transport, and other infrastructure needed to accommodate large numbers of visitors. Potential destinations may also lack the private sector capacity, qualified workforce, or promotional expertise to make tourism investments succeed. Even Brazil, with its vast land area and high tourism potential, spent only an estimated 2 percent of its budget on tourism-related activities in 2000, well below the world average of more than 5 percent.[36]

Certain developing countries remain almost completely marginalized from tourism, facing serious geographic and political obstacles to its development. The South Pacific island of Kiribati, for example, is remote from other tourist centers, while Solomon Islands and Vanuatu are vulnerable to hurricanes, earthquakes, and other natural disasters. And the tourism industry of Sierra Leone, after experiencing a decade of strong growth, all but collapsed in the late 1990s as a result of that country's civil war and economic decline.[37]

Yet even in developing countries that do attract growing numbers of visitors, the on-the-ground benefits of tourism are not always as significant as they might appear. Indeed, these benefits have generally failed to reach those segments of the world's population—such as the very poor—that could gain the most from them. This is in part because governments and donors have largely viewed tourism as a vehicle to win foreign exchange earnings and investment, and less as a tool to achieve broader social and economic objectives, such as strengthening local economies and alleviating poverty.[38]

This outlook is beginning to change as institutions like the World Bank and the World Tourism Organization reorient their funding and technical assistance. According to Sheryl Spivack, associate professor of tourism studies at George Washington University, the World Tourism Organization has moved forward in recent years, "not only better assessing the economic impact of tourism, but finding creative ways to help communities understand the importance of making tourism a sound and beneficial development option."[39]

But progress has been slow. The continuing reality is that a large share of the tourism revenue that enters developing countries does not remain in the local or national economy, where it could be used to support families and boost basic services such as health care or education. Often, the money goes to urban elites or ends up outside the country. The World Tourism Organization estimates that on average as much as 50 percent of tourism earnings ultimately "leak" out of the developing world—in the form of profits earned by foreign-owned businesses, promotional spending abroad, or payments for imported goods and labor. The share of leakage ranges from as little as 10 percent in more advanced and diversified economies to as much as 75 percent in smaller, more dependent economies.[40]

Leakage is particularly high in the Caribbean, where 50–70 percent of tourism earnings go toward acquiring imports—from skilled staff to food and consumer goods. Many hotels and other tourism businesses rely heavily on foreign imports and workers, either because the luxury goods and services that tourists demand are not available domestically, or because the tourism sector is so poorly linked with other sectors like fishing, agriculture, manufacturing, and transport that it is difficult to procure local supplies.[41]

To slow at least some of the revenue loss, governments could work to strengthen linkages among diverse economic sectors and to stimulate the growth of domestically owned tourism enterprises. Yet many governments are under growing pressure to grant outside investors—including large international hotel chains, airlines, and tour operators—easier access to tourism assets. Under a special economic relations treaty with the United States, for example, Thailand is obligated to grant companies owned and operated by U.S. investors the same legal treatment as those owned by Thai nationals. Across the developing world, the increase in foreign investments, mergers, and franchising arrangements threatens to crowd out smaller, local businesses that are unable to compete.[42]

Foreign-based operators dominate the tourism industries of many countries, including Kenya, Tanzania, and Zimbabwe. These businesses typically send their profits back home, leaving little revenue at the destination. Meanwhile, the bulk of a tourist's spending, including the biggest purchases like airline tickets, tour packages, and rental cars, occurs in the home country and never even reaches the destination. According to one estimate, if both the hotel and airline are foreign-owned, as much as 80 percent of a traveler's fees are lost to these businesses. Cruise vacations and other all-inclusive tour packages that cover not only airfare, lodging, and transport but also documentation fees, entertainment, and meals often siphon off the largest share of the tourism dollar.[43]

The Central American nation of Belize, which has seen rapid tourism growth in recent years, has experienced many of these problems. In the early 1990s, expatriates accounted for roughly 65 percent of the membership in the Belize Tourism Industry Association, and an estimated 90 percent of the country's coastal development was in foreign hands.

Many Belizeans oppose the rapid growth in luxury resorts and villas, but they are unlikely to be able to buy the land back. Meanwhile, the presence of foreign investments, together with the higher purchasing power of tourists, has boosted local inflation, raising property and food prices.[44]

Some countries are working to spread the benefits of tourism more broadly, however. On the Caribbean island of Dominica, restrictions on foreign ownership give residents greater control of the land, and more than 62 percent of facilities and 70 percent of accommodation units are locally owned. Meanwhile, the island of Saint Lucia, where more than 60 percent of tourist lodging has traditionally been in large all-inclusive hotels, is making a concerted effort to support smaller-scale local tourism enterprise. In 1998, the government launched a "heritage tourism" initiative that provides grants, training, and technical assistance to help entrepreneurs develop cultural tours and other businesses in their own rural and coastal communities.[45]

> **The struggle over tourism ownership will . . . intensify as countries . . . give greater advantage to foreign investors.**

The struggle over tourism ownership will likely intensify as countries implement new international trade and investment policies that give greater advantage to foreign investors. Under the General Agreement on Trade in Services (GATS), a 1994 multilateral trade agreement aimed at liberalizing service industries, member countries must give equal market opportunity to service providers from other signatory nations—including foreign tourism businesses like hotels, restaurants, travel agencies, tour operations, and guide services. GATS requires governments to remove subsidies and protections on local enterprises and makes it considerably easier for foreign businesses to establish franchises, transfer staff, and repatriate profits. So far, at least 112 countries are committed to opening up their tourism markets under GATS—more than are pledged to open up any other economic sector—suggesting strong international interest in stimulating tourism investments. A second trade measure, the Agreement on Trade Related Investment Measures (TRIMS), makes it harder for governments to require foreign companies to use local materials and inputs.[46]

The employment effects of tourism are also mixed. As a service industry, tourism has great potential to bring jobs and income to disadvantaged groups, such as the poor and women. According to the World Travel and Tourism Council, roughly 65 percent of the positions created by tourism annually are found in the developing world. Not surprisingly, tourism employs the most people in heavily populated countries like China and India, at 48 million and 18 million, respectively. But it accounts for the highest share of total employment in small island countries like the Bahamas, the Maldives, and Saint Lucia, where more than 45 percent of jobs are tourism-related. On the island of Anguilla, the figure nears 65 percent (compared with only 9 percent in Japan).[47]

People find formal employment in resorts, restaurants, travel agencies, and tour companies, as well as positions in tourism-related sectors like construction and agriculture. Carolyn Cain, a consultant for the International Finance Corporation, estimates that each hotel room built can create one to two new jobs on average. Many of these positions go to women: on average, women account for 46 percent of workers in the hotel, catering, and restaurant sectors—a much higher share than in labor markets overall. (See Box 1.) Women also do much of the informal tourism work, such as running food stalls and selling crafts.[48]

For many people, especially those in rural areas, working in tourism provides a welcome alternative to joblessness, bringing in money for basic needs. But more often than not, foreign or city-based workers hold the more lucrative management positions in tourism, leaving residents with service jobs—porters, maids, or laborers—that are low-wage and offer little opportunity for skill building. The International Labour Organisation (ILO) reports that tourism workers earn 20 percent less on average than workers in other economic sectors. And many of these positions do not meet international labor

BOX 1

Tourism and the Employment of Women

Tourism is an increasingly important source of livelihood for women in the developing world. Many tourism jobs are flexible or part-time positions that do not require much training, enabling the participation of poorer and less educated women. Tourism also offers opportunities for self-employment, as well as informal opportunities like vending food and crafts.

Yet women often face the same obstacles working in tourism as they do in other labor markets. The majority of workers hold low-wage domestic positions—such as housekeeping, cooking, and waitressing—that offer little job security, opportunity for advancement, or skill development. At worst, many desperate women end up in demoralizing and dangerous work, such as prostitution.

However, tourism can be an important vehicle for alleviating poverty and empowering women. Around the world, groups are working to enhance women's participation in tourism by providing basic training in finance, marketing, and language and offering microcredit loans to facilitate access to capital. With independence, women are better able to launch their own tourism businesses, from craft cooperatives to catering and accommodation. One traditional guesthouse started by a local woman in Bali, Indonesia, offers cooking courses for guests and provides education and skill development to its employees, many of whom are women. The project also contributes tourist donations to help build roads, houses, and temples, and to support local schools.

Another successful women's project is the Siyabonga Craft Cooperative, launched in South Africa's KwaZulu-Natal forest. The surrounding community has traditionally benefited only marginally from booming tourism in the region, and in 1995 unemployment among economically active women topped 42 percent. That year, a group of local women approached the Natal Parks Board for funding to build a permanent craft cooperative to replace the haphazard system of roadside stalls they had been using to market their products. Today, 10 percent of the profits from sales of the crafts—most of which are harvested sustainably from the forest—go to shop expenses, while the rest goes toward meeting members' basic needs and educating their children. The enterprise has also strengthened the women's confidence and organizational and entrepreneurial skills, spurring several of them to seek further schooling.

Source: See endnote 48.

standards: some 13–19 million children under the age of 18 now work in tourism, roughly 2 million of whom have been lured into the booming "sex tourism" industries of Southeast Asia and Latin America, where they risk exposure to HIV/AIDS and other sexually transmitted diseases.[49]

Tourism can also divert people from traditional jobs in agriculture and fishing, tightening the local labor supply and increasing dependence on imports. In Nepal, for instance, the boom in the trekking industry has reportedly caused a shortage of agricultural labor. And in Grenada, the government is replacing small-scale, organic agricultural plots with large tourism resorts, squeezing out local farmers in a push to secure foreign investment. The same thing is happening to local agriculture at destinations from Jerba, Tunisia, to Goa, India.[50]

If economies become too narrowly dependent on tourism, however, they are more vulnerable to a collapse resulting from changing tourist tastes or other factors, including fear of international terrorism. Indeed, tourism workers were among the first to feel the effects of global insecurity and economic downturn following the September 2001 attacks in the United States. Within weeks, the French tour operator Club Méditerranée had announced the winter closure of 15 of its resort villages in 10 countries in the Caribbean, Central America, Africa, the Middle East, Europe, and Asia. In total, the ILO estimated that as many as 9 million tourism workers would lose their jobs in the wake of the attacks—with nearly three quarters of these losses outside the United States and Europe.[51]

Tourism also has varied impacts on local cultures. On the one hand, it can heighten national respect for minorities and indigenous groups, helping to sustain or revive languages, religious traditions, and other practices that might otherwise be lost. In Bali, Indonesia, for instance, tourist demand for dancing and other arts has fostered an artistic revival—even though many dancers now perform in hotels rather than in the traditional palaces and temples. And rising interest in alternative healing worldwide has spurred a resurgence of shamanism in Peru. Mateo Arevalo, a long-time shaman from the country's Shipibo community, now brings in as much as $30 per tourist for performing a one-night ceremony and earns $200 a month hosting foreign students in his home.[52]

Yet many indigenous communities end up the "featured attractions" of ventures they have had limited or no input in designing, leaving them little opportunity to accept or reject the changes that tourism brings. The reduction of entire cultures to brochure snapshots can lead visitors to view residents as oddities rather than as people. As Guatemalan native and Nobel Peace Prize laureate Rigoberta Menchu once explained, "What hurts Indians most is that our costumes are considered beautiful, but it's as if the person wearing it didn't exist." Turning serious rituals and festivals into tourist commodities can ultimately affect community self-perception and behavior. In the Himalayas, rising tourist interest in Buddhist festivals has led monks to shorten elaborate rituals to satisfy tourist attention spans and has spurred a black market in religious artwork. Meanwhile, local involvement in the events has dropped off.[53]

In general, it is difficult to distinguish the changes that tourism brings to communities from the wider effects of globalization, westernization, and rising economic prosperity. But tourism can accelerate the influx of western values and material goods into indigenous areas, spurring changes in eating, dress, and other daily activities. Forest tribes in Peru can now earn more selling traditional cloaks to tourists than trading them for axes or machetes—a shift that has reportedly altered the economic relations of villages.[54]

In extreme cases, native communities have been forcefully evicted from their homelands to make room for tourists. In the 1950s, Kenya's colonial government drove the nomadic Masai from their traditional grazing lands to accommodate safari lodges and visitors to the newly created national parks and wildlife sanctuaries. The Masai have since won greater involvement in the management and use of their resources, and have been able to meet community needs with money earned from leasing their land. Yet they still face the social and cultural repercussions of tourism, including misrepresentation of their crafts and rituals and a rising incidence of prostitution, alcoholism, and drug use. More recently, Burmese authorities gave the 5,200 residents of the ancient Buddhist city of Pagan only two weeks notice before evicting them in 1990 and turning the pagodas where they lived into a tourist attraction.[55]

Despite the potential negative impacts, many communities still favor increased tourism because they see economic and cultural opportunities that outweigh the drawbacks. Indigenous groups like Ecuador's Cofan and Huaorani have actively organized their own tourism operations, setting up guest lodges and craft shops that represent a less resource-intensive source of revenue than oil development. Panama's Kuna people also hope to maximize the benefits of tourism while fighting some of the unwelcome changes. Their Statute on Tourism, ratified in 1996, limits the number of hotels yet ensures the collection of tax revenue and the redistribution of benefits among community members.[56]

Environmental Impacts Of Tourism

As soaring air travel brings many of Earth's most ecologically fragile destinations within easy reach, concern about tourism's environmental impacts is rising. Travelers from industrial countries often try to replicate their own high-consumption lifestyles at their destinations, increasing pressures on ecosystems and resources. Yet few developing-country governments have the capacity to protect their attractions adequately from all these new visitors.[57]

Tourism's environmental impacts can begin even before arrival. Studies suggest that as much as 90 percent of a tourist's energy consumption is spent getting to and from the destination. Increasingly, the passenger jet, the most polluting form of transport per kilometer traveled, is overtaking the automobile as the primary means of tourist travel: an estimated 43 percent of international tourists now fly to their destinations, while 42 percent travel by road and 15 percent go by either rail or ship. Air travel has been particularly important in the developing world, where in some countries at least 90 percent of tourists arrive by plane.[58]

Unfortunately, air transport is one of the world's fastest-growing sources of emissions of carbon dioxide and other greenhouse gases responsible for global climate change. The Intergovernmental Panel on Climate Change reports that aircraft emissions contributed roughly 3.5 percent of human-generated greenhouse gases in 1992—and this share is expected to rise steadily as air travel increases. (See Figure 4.)[59]

Ironically, rising carbon emissions from air travel and other sources could end up hurting many of the world's top tourism destinations. In a 1999 report for the World Wide Fund for Nature UK, authors David Viner and Maureen Agnew warn that soaring temperatures, forest fires, and other consequences of global warming could drive wildlife from safari parks in southern and eastern Africa, damage Brazil's rainforest ecosystems, foster malaria in the Mediterranean, and flood beaches and coastal destinations worldwide. Already, rising sea levels and coral bleaching events linked to warming temperatures are threatening the economies of low-lying tropical islands like Maldives, where tourism generates more than 85 percent of foreign exchange receipts and reefs attract 40 percent of all visitors.[60]

Once tourists arrive at their destinations, their choices of where to sleep, eat, shop, and be entertained increasingly come at the expense of the environment. Natural and rural landscapes are rapidly being converted to roads, airports, hotels, gift shops, parking lots, and other facilities, leading to deterioration of the sites that attract tourists in the first place. Although new infrastructure, such as a road, may have only a minor initial impact on an area, it can ultimately open a region to large-scale development. The Southern African Research Documentation Centre has warned of an impending ecological

FIGURE 4

International Passenger Air Traffic, 1950-2000

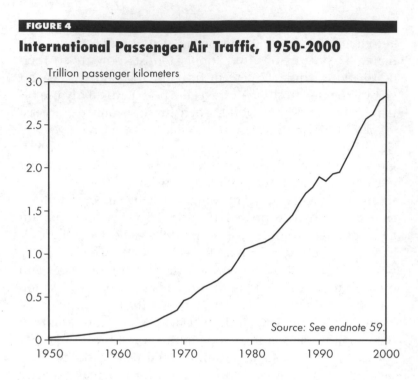

disaster at the world-renowned Victoria Falls, shared by Zimbabwe and Zambia, where a new multimillion-dollar hotel was recently built only a few meters from the water. Already, the Zambezi River is polluted with detergents, uncollected garbage, and human waste from existing hotels—the result of poor regional tourism planning.[61]

Hotel and resort construction accounts for a growing share of tourism's environmental impact, and the trend is toward larger hotels, particularly in the newer destinations. The number of hotel rooms worldwide increased by more than 25 percent between 1990 and 1998, reaching an estimated 15 million. Regionally, South Asia has witnessed the fastest hotel growth, though Europe and the Americas still boast the highest share of rooms overall, at 38 percent and 34 percent of the total, respectively. Significant hotel and resort construction has also occurred in Caribbean countries like Barbados and Antigua and Barbuda.[62]

In her book *Last Resorts: The Cost of Tourism in the Caribbean*, author Polly Pattullo describes how coastal construction methods like sand mining and dredge-and-fill have destroyed dunes and wetlands, caused groundwater supplies to become brackish, and stirred up nearby waters—choking coral reefs and diminishing fish populations. In Cancun, Mexico, large swaths of mangrove forests, salt marshes, and other wetland areas that harbor wildlife and protect coral reefs have been cleared and filled to make room for resorts, piers, and marinas. These areas are often shored up with topsoil scraped from wetland savanna areas inland, resulting in the disruption of two valuable ecosystems. Developers are currently building some 21 new resort complexes along Mexico's Yucatán coast—a construction frenzy that is expected to nearly triple the number of area hotel rooms to 24,000.[63]

The world's hotels and their guests consume massive quantities of resources on a daily basis, including energy for heating and cooling rooms, lighting hallways, and cooking meals, as well as water for washing laundry, filling swimming pools, and watering golf courses. This resource use is not only expensive—in the United States, the average laundry cost per occupied room is almost $3.50 a day—but it can also damage the environment. According to one estimate, a tourist spending a two-week vacation at a resort hotel can use more than 100 kilograms of fossil fuels.[64]

In Israel, heavy water use by hotels and other tourist facilities along the Jordan River and other tributaries is contributing to the drying up of the Dead Sea. Water levels have dropped by an estimated 40 meters over the last 50 years, leaving barren, salty mudflats that are hostile to native plants and birds. Environmentalists predict that at current rates of diversion, the Dead Sea could disappear completely by 2050.[65]

Heavy promotion of golf tourism at many resort destinations has intensified water shortages, particularly in Asia. Each year, up to 5,000 hectares of the Earth's land surface— an area half the size of Paris—are cleared for golf courses, and one 18-hole course can consume more than 2.3 million liters of water daily. One popular course on an island in Malaysia uses as much water annually as a local village of 20,000.[66]

At destinations where freshwater is scarce, overconsumption by tourists and tourism facilities can divert supplies from local residents or farmers, exacerbating shortages and raising utility prices. Tourists in Grenada generally use seven times as much water as local people, and foreign-owned hotels tend to receive preference over residents during droughts. Similarly, the World Wide Fund for Nature estimates that the average Mediterranean tourist uses nearly four times as much water as the average Spaniard, an estimated 880 liters per day. In the Philippines, the diversion of water to tourist lodges and restaurants threatens to destroy paddy irrigation at the 3,000-year-old Banaue rice terraces, a unique cultural heritage site.[67]

In addition to consuming water, energy, and other resources, tourism creates large quantities of waste. The U.N. Environment Programme (UNEP) estimates that the average tourist produces roughly one kilogram of solid waste and litter each day. Hotels, swimming pools, golf courses, marinas, and other facilities also generate a wide variety of harmful residues on a daily basis, among them synthetic chemicals, oil, nutrients, and pathogens. Improperly disposed of, this waste can damage nearby ecosystems, contaminating water sources and harming wildlife.[68]

Many tourist facilities in the developing world possess limited or no sewage treatment facilities, in part because of weak environmental legislation or a lack of money, monitoring equipment, and trained staff. As recently as 1990, none of the 22,000 beachfront hotel rooms in Pattaya, Thailand, were attached to a sewage plant; as of 1996, only 60 percent of that city's sewage was being processed. And a 1994 study for the Caribbean Tourism Organization reported that hotels in that region released some 80–90 percent of their sewage in coastal waters, near hotels, on beaches, and around coral reefs and mangroves without adequate treatment.[69]

Cruise ships are notorious for their waste disposal problems. Worldwide, the number of people taking cruises nearly doubled between 1990 and 1999, to 9 million passengers annually. The San Francisco-based Bluewater Network reports that on a one-week voyage, a typical cruise ship generates some 3.8 million liters of graywater (water from sinks, showers, and laundry); 795,000 liters of sewage; 95,000 liters of oily bilge water; eight tons of garbage; 416 liters of photo chemicals; and 19 liters of dry cleaning waste. Many older vessels have little alternative to dumping this waste overboard. According to one estimate, the world's cruise ships discharge some 90,000 tons of raw sewage and garbage into the oceans each day.[70]

Cruise operators also dump an untold amount of waste illegally to avoid having to store it on board or to pay for costly disposal on land. In one highly publicized case, Royal Caribbean Cruises received a record $18 million fine in 1999 for 21 counts of discharging excess oily bilge and other pollutants into U.S. waters and then attempting to cover up its crime.[71]

These problems will likely persist as shipbuilders rush to meet the rising demand for cruise vacations. In 2001, at least 53 new vessels were on the order books. Many newer ships resemble "floating cities," boasting more than 2,000 passengers and up to 1,000 crew members. One company is currently building an eight-story, 250,000-ton ship capable of carrying 6,200 passengers. To accommodate these larger vessels, countries often dredge deep-water harbors or modify their coastlines, destroying coastal ecosystems in the process. When ships dock, their massive anchors and chains can break coral heads and devastate underwater habitats. In 1994, one local scientist in the Cayman Islands reported that more than 120 hectares of reefs had been lost as a result of cruise ship anchoring in George Town harbor.[72]

Busloads of cruise passengers, day-trippers, and other visitors are overwhelming fragile cultural and natural sites that are ill equipped to manage rising tourist numbers. UNESCO reports that the number of tourists ascending the

Inca Trail to Peru's Machu Picchu ruins increased from only 6,000 in 1984 to 66,000 in 1998. And visits to Cambodia's ancient Angkor temples more than doubled in 1999 following the government's decision to open the nearby town to international flights—intensifying wear on the already fragile stone structures.[73]

Popular natural sites are also beginning to suffer. Plastic water bottles, soda cans, and gum wrappers litter the trails of Malaysia's largest national park, Taman Negara, where tourism has more than tripled over the past 10 years. In safari parks in Kenya and Tanzania, tourist vehicles destroy grass cover, while visitors and staff fell forests adjacent to lodges and campgrounds to obtain fuelwood. And Costa Rica had to close off parts of the popular Manuel Antonio National Park to prevent it from being overwhelmed with visitors and their trash.[74]

The presence of tourists in natural areas can also negatively affect wildlife behavior and populations. Around the world, whalewatching boats relentlessly pursue whales and dolphins and even encourage petting, altering the animals' feeding and social activity. In the Caribbean, some sharks, manatees, and other marine species have lost their natural fear of people because tour guides feed them to ensure that they will remain in tourist areas. And in Africa's parks, tourist vehicles that approach cheetahs, lions, and other animals often distract these creatures from breeding or stalking their prey. Safari tourists are also one of the top markets for illegal elephant ivory, which is banned under international law yet often sold to unsuspecting tourists in the form of souvenir carvings.[75]

At particularly fragile destinations, such as small islands, it can take relatively few visitors to leave a mark. Tourists may unintentionally trample vegetation, disturb nesting seabirds, breeding seals, or other animals, and bring invasive plants and animals in with their equipment or luggage. The introduction of these "exotic" species threatens to destroy the unique flora and fauna of Ecuador's Galapagos Islands, where tourism has increased by 66 percent since

1990 and where the local population—attracted by tourism's potential—has doubled in the past 15 years.[76]

In mountain areas, resorts and related infrastructure can disrupt animal migration, divert water from streams, create waste that is difficult to dispose of at high altitudes, and deforest hillsides, triggering landslides. In one Nepalese mountain village, an estimated hectare of virgin rhododendron forest is cut down each year for fuelwood to support the country's booming trekking industry, leading to the erosion of some 30–75 tons of soil annually. And in Tanzania, the number of trekkers on the trails of Mount Kilimanjaro has risen so dramatically that the government doubled the daily climbing fee to $100 per person in September 1999 to slow serious erosion and other environmental harm.[77]

Busloads of cruise passengers, day-trippers, and other visitors are overwhelming fragile sites . . . .

In coastal areas, popular recreational activities such as scuba diving, snorkeling, and sport fishing are damaging coral reefs and other marine resources—though this destruction is minor compared with the impacts of coral bleaching, overfishing, and ocean pollution. UNEP estimates that each year some 300,000 scuba diving trips are advertised to the world's estimated 6 million divers. With their fins and hands, divers and snorkelers have broken as many as 10 percent of coral colonies at certain popular Red Sea reefs off Egypt and Israel. A study of self-guided snorkel trails in Australia found similar damage at sites visited by an average of only 15 snorkelers per week. And research off the Caribbean island of Bonaire reveals that heavy diving at many sites has changed the composition of reefs, with more opportunistic, branching corals taking the place of older coral colonies. Souvenir shops and restaurants around the world also contribute to the destruction, as reefs are looted for shells, coral, and seafood to meet tourist demand.[78]

Not surprisingly, this behavior can ultimately hurt the tourism industry, destroying the very reefs, beaches, forests, and other attractions that lure visitors in the first place. Tourism researchers often refer to the "life-cycle" of a destination—its evolution from discovery, to development, to eventual decline. More often than not, the final stage of decline is attributed to a site's overuse and the subsequent deterioration of key attractions or facilities.[79]

If the loss in environmental quality is significant enough, a destination may begin to lose revenue, as happened in Kovalam in India or in Barbados after the 1980s. Many places in the industrial world have already lost tourists or are expected to soon due to environmental degradation, including Germany's Black Forest and Italy's Adriatic coast. Environmental deterioration also continues to impede efforts to boost tourism to many cities in the developing world: Cairo's urban sprawl, for instance, often alienates visitors, as do the mounting gridlock and pollution in places like Bangkok and Beijing.[80]

Ecotourism: Friend or Foe?

Over the past decade or so, tourism authorities and businesses, environmentalists, and academics have embraced ecotourism as a way to address some of tourism's negative impacts while generating foreign exchange, creating jobs, and stimulating investment. One non-profit organization that promotes ecotourism, the Vermont-based International Ecotourism Society, defines it as "responsible travel to natural areas that conserves the environment and sustains the well-being of local people." The United Nations has demonstrated its support for the concept by declaring 2002 the International Year of Ecotourism.[81]

But whether ecotourism can really achieve its ambitious goals remains to be seen. In some cases, it appears to be working. A wide variety of lodges, tour operations, and other enterprises that operate in natural settings are making significant efforts to minimize their environmental and social impacts. Many have developed or support initiatives to protect local ecosystems, wildlife, and cultures.[82]

Yet as worldwide interest in visiting jungles, beaches, waterfalls, and other natural attractions continues to grow, the ecotourism concept is increasingly being corrupted. To cash in on the trend, growing numbers of less responsible hotels and tour operators—from one-person snorkeling operations in Belize to luxurious lodges on Africa's savannahs— now bill themselves as ecotourism outfits. One operator in Cusco, Peru, estimates that less than 10 percent of the local trekking companies really fit the "eco" bill. In the absence of a universal ecotourism standard, it is increasingly difficult to distinguish these less responsible businesses from more genuine ecotourism operations. Meanwhile, many industry promoters and tourists themselves now call any travel that occurs in nature "ecotourism," blurring the line between genuine ecotourism and nature travel more broadly.[83]

Ecotourism, broadly defined, is one of the fastest-growing segments of the tourism industry. Though the varying definitions make it difficult to measure, the International Ecotourism Society estimates that this form of travel is growing by 20 percent annually (compared with 7 percent for tourism overall) and that it generated some $154 billion in receipts in 2000. One 1992 study found that as many as 60 percent of international tourists traveled to experience and enjoy nature, while as many as 40 percent traveled specifically to observe wildlife, such as birds and whales. The $1 billion-a-year whalewatching industry now attracts some 9 million visitors in 87 countries, up from 4 million in 31 countries in 1991.[84]

Most of the demand for ecotourism originates in North America and Europe. A 1992 survey by the U.S. Travel Data Center found that 7 percent of U.S. travelers, or some 8 million people, had taken at least one ecotourism trip (defined as travel where visitors learn about and appreciate the environment), while another 30 percent—35 million people—planned to take one during the next three years. Factors behind this rising demand include a desire to experience new and pristine places, learn about different cultures and environments, and face recreational challenges.[85]

The earliest ecotourists traveled to Africa to view elephants, lions, and other wildlife in the big game parks of Kenya, Tanzania, and South Africa. Today, popular activities also include trekking in the Himalayas, hiking in the rainforests of Central and South America, and scuba diving and snorkeling in Southeast Asia and the Caribbean. The Caribbean alone is home to nearly 60 percent of the world's scuba tours. This demand is expected to continue well into the century: the World Tourism Organization predicts that the trendiest destinations of the future will be "the tops of the highest mountains, the depths of the oceans, and the ends of the earth." [86]

Rising interest in ecotourism has had many positive benefits. For example, governments have set aside valuable natural areas as national parks or protected areas, thus sparing them from more environmentally destructive activities such as agriculture, logging, or mining. Laurent Belsie, writing in the *Christian Science Monitor*, explains that "tourist dollars, rather than lectures on the environmental importance of saving the rainforest, speak volumes in many of the developing world's parliaments and presidential palaces." [87]

Some of the greatest increases in ecotourism have occurred in places with the highest numbers of protected areas. In 1997, an estimated 60 percent of the nearly 6 million tourists who visited South Africa stopped at a national park or reserve. And nearly half of all respondents in a survey of tourists in Central America cited protected areas as an important factor in choosing their destination.[88]

Once they have established parks and reserves, however, not all governments are willing or able to pay for the upkeep. Worldwide, financial support for these areas is dwindling. While many governments hope to use tourist admission fees and donations to boost park management,

strengthen infrastructure, and protect against encroach-
ment, this self-financing mechanism has been more successful in some areas than others. (See Box 2.)[89]

As an alternative, many countries are actively wooing
private tourism investments to help protect natural areas.
Brazil, Chile, Colombia, Kenya, and South Africa have all
witnessed an explosion in the number of privately owned
nature reserves, many of which open their lodges and trails
to tourists. Two private reserves in
Central America—Costa Rica's **Some of the great-**
Monteverde Cloud Forest and Belize's
Community Baboon Sanctuary—are **est increases in**
well managed and generate sufficient **ecotourism have**
income from tourist fees to maintain
themselves properly. In a survey of 32 **occurred in places**
private reserves in Latin America and **with the highest**
sub-Saharan Africa, researcher Jeff **numbers of**
Langholz found that the majority
were profitable and that their overall **protected areas.**
profitability had risen 21 percent
since 1989. On average, tourism revenues provided more than
67 percent of reserve income.[90]

Some eco-resorts display a high level of environmental
commitment, carefully monitoring visitor impacts as well as
their own ecological and social footprints. The most basic
lodges are fueled by propane, kerosene, solar, or wind energy rather than electricity or fuelwood, use no indoor plumb-
ing, and generate minimal waste. The Sí Como No resort, in
Costa Rica's popular Manuel Antonio National Park, for example, relies on solar energy, uses aerial bridges instead of roads
or walkways, puts in native plants to halt erosion, sponsors
beach cleanups, and asks guests to reuse sheets and towels.[91]

But not all private ecotourism investments are conservation oriented. Many countries are actively wooing the private sector and lending institutions like the IFC to bring
private restaurants, lodges, and other facilities to natural
areas as a way to generate revenue. But the rising commercial
presence of large hotels, restaurants, and other concessions

BOX 2

Can Ecotourism Pay Its Way?

As government funding for parks and protected areas dwindles, more and more natural sites in the developing world are relying on tourist dollars to support themselves. The Bonaire Marine Park in the Caribbean, for example, began collecting a $10 fee from visiting divers and snorkelers in 1991. Within a year, the park had raised enough money from the program to cover annual operation and maintenance costs.

Yet this self-financing does not work everywhere. In Costa Rica, visitor fees provide only about a quarter of the park service's annual budget for management and protection; the rest must be raised from donations. And tourism revenue at Indonesia's Komodo National Park covered only about 7 percent of total park expenditure in the early 1990s.

In some cases, no tourist dollars are reinvested in conservation or park management, going instead to central government coffers or corrupt park authorities. For example, not a single cent of the $3.7 million that tourists paid to visit the islands off Mexico's Baja Peninsula in 1993 went directly to the protection or management of these areas.

In other instances, authorities charge woefully low admission, or else demand no fees at all out of a fear that this will deter tourists. Yet studies show that tourists are willing to pay much more than they do to visit natural areas. Surveys in the United States found that 63 percent of travelers would pay up to $50 toward conservation in the area visited, while 27 percent would pay as much as $200. Studies at Komodo National Park suggest that visitors there would pay up to 10 times the current entry fee.

The few sites that do charge much higher fees and apply them to conservation and management are benefiting greatly, particularly when the system allows for different rates for tourists and local people. Ecuador's Galapagos National Park has reportedly recouped nine times its management costs by charging foreign visitors $100. And gorilla viewing—at $250 a day—subsidized all 11 of Uganda's national parks in the late 1990s, providing 70 percent of park system revenue.

Yet some ecotourism sites may never see enough visitors to support themselves, even with higher fees. Studies in Central Africa's Dzangha-Sangha protected area suggest that tourism would have to increase nearly eightfold to generate a positive return on investment—a near impossibility, even if entry fees jumped from $16 to $200.

Source: See endnote 89.

near or inside park boundaries threatens to destroy natural settings in many destinations. China, for instance, is aggressively transferring control of its important scenic and cultural sites to private development companies, who then profit from their monopolies by charging admission fees and collecting revenues from hotels, restaurants, and gift shops. In some instances, the environment has also benefited: at the scenic mountain site of Huangsan, litter is now virtually nonexistent and forest cover has increased markedly since the 1980s. But two planned hotels and three new cable car runs, as well as increased pedestrian traffic, could ultimately destroy ecosystems in the area.[92]

Unregulated and poorly planned ecotourism can bring high levels of environmental destruction by both tourism operators and tourists. One critic, Anita Pleumarom of Thailand's Tourism Investigation and Monitoring Team, alleges that the rampant construction of large resorts in ecologically sensitive areas enables politicians, developers, and others to increasingly gain commercial access to these areas and to accelerate the privatization of biological diversity. This concern is not entirely unfounded: in recent years, there have been reports of scientists, students, and researchers who have attempted to patent local medicinal plants gathered during "ecotourism" trips in Viet Nam and elsewhere.[93]

Moreover, as ecotourism enters the mainstream, it increasingly faces many of the same problems as conventional tourism. Just like conventional tourists, ecotourists fly long distances to their destinations and require food, lodging, and other basics, consuming resources and producing waste. As Geoffrey Wall, professor of geography at the University of Waterloo in Canada, puts it, "Visitors are encouraged to take only photographs and leave only footprints. However, even footprints make their mark." The earliest ecotourists often had little choice but to take local transport and stay in locally run accommodations. But today, growing numbers of ecotourists are creating the demand for higher-end facilities, many of which leave a greater environmental impact.[94]

And like conventional tourists, many ecotourists make their travel, tour, and accommodation plans with companies back home, spending the bulk of their travel budget outside the destination. Before violence put a halt to Rwanda's tourism in the mid-1990s, international airlines were making an estimated $10 million a year from visitors to the country's Mountain Gorilla Project alone.[95]

At the same time, while many early ecotourists were motivated by a keen environmental and political awareness, not all of today's ecotourists are as environmentally minded, or are prompted by a desire to learn about and respect nature. Indeed, as author Martha Honey observes, today's ecotourists are "less intellectually curious, socially responsible, environmentally concerned, and politically aware" than those in the past. Survey research in Australia's Northern Territory confirms this observation, suggesting that many travelers see ecotourism as simply another form of tourist consumerism or a relaxing holiday experience. Many are just after new destinations to visit and have no deeper interest in the site—a phenomenon researcher Erlet Cater calls the "this year the Galapagos next year Antarctica" syndrome. Because their trips are often only a week or even a day long, these tourists may not consider the repercussions of their visits, or feel the need to follow every rule.[96]

In few places is the risk of "mass" ecotourism more apparent than in Costa Rica, once a little-known tropical destination. It has become so popular that new airports, beachfront resorts, golf courses, and marinas are being built to accommodate the more than 700,000 tourists who arrive annually, endangering the lush rainforests and other natural sites that they come to see. Other countries, from Thailand to South Africa, are seeing a similar surge in tourist numbers to their natural settings.[97]

There are significant efforts to promote a more genuine form of ecotourism that requires less land and resources, generates less waste and pollution, and brings benefits to both local communities and the environment. Initiatives that are either managed by the community or that share a substantial portion of their profits with local residents can be particularly successful at achieving these goals. They can range from small-scale, low-impact efforts like offering an extra room or meal, renting out a small cabana, or showcasing traditional dances, to larger-scale investments like eco-lodges or canopy walkways. Homegrown ecotourism initiatives generally require less infrastructure and overhead than larger tourism projects and rely more heavily on goods, materials, and staff from the surrounding area.[98]

Although all residents do not necessarily benefit, such initiatives can help to spread tourism's benefits more widely. Because ecotourism takes place primarily in rural or less developed areas where poor and indigenous people live, it can bring greater attention, resources, and employment to these groups. In Ecuador's Amazon Basin, for example, the Cofan people offer guest cabins and a craft shop that together generate some $500 per resident annually. Another Ecuadorian group, the Huaorani, have set up a community project that evenly distributes nightly tourist fees among all the families and earns residents twice what they would get working for an oil company.[99]

A high level of local participation is desirable not only because it can reduce revenue leakage, but also because it can heighten local appreciation for wildlife and other natural resources. One Ugandan farmer, talking about the recent boost in gorilla-related tourism at the nearby Budongo Forest Reserve, remarked of the benefits, "We never thought that vermin like these monkeys could become a source of money...now they pay for our schools." When communities see direct benefits from tourism, they are more likely to slow resource use and to actively protect natural areas. Subsistence farmers participating in Zimbabwe's 23-district CAMPFIRE project recognize that they can earn three times more from offering wildlife viewing, sustainable safari hunting, and other tourism-related activities on their land than from resource-intensive cattle ranching. And people living near Nepal's Sagarmatha National Park reportedly slowed their indiscriminate tree felling in response to increased trekking tourism.[100]

Across the developing world, growing numbers of poachers and other resource users are becoming tour guides, applying their wide understanding of local natural history and culture to tourist needs. Former fishers from Belize's small island of Caye Caulker, for instance, now use their knowledge of marine life to guide snorkelers and divers through the nearby Hol Chan Marine Reserve. Worldwide, longtime whalers now lead whalewatching trips and former hunters guide jungle and river tours. With so much time invested in tourism, and with more income, many of these individuals no longer need to hunt or pursue other resource-intensive activities.[101]

Alternatively, studies show that when tourism initiatives exclude local people from participating in the management and use of natural areas where they grow food, raise livestock, and gather fuel, they are more likely to resent these efforts and seek to undermine them, ultimately compromising conservation goals. Areas that exclude local participation and use have seen rising incidences of poaching, vandalism, and even armed conflict. One Galapagos fisher reportedly said of government efforts to limit local use of the park's resources: "If the government does not lift the fishing ban we are even willing to burn all the natural areas to finish this tourism craziness."[102]

Many local ecotourism initiatives have benefited from partnerships with outsiders, including government agencies, the private sector, and nongovernmental organizations. One Virginia-based non-profit, the RARE Center for Tropical Conservation, instructs former hunters, fishers, and other resource users in Latin America, Asia, and Africa in conversational English, local natural history, interpretation, and guiding. To date, RARE has trained more than 200 guides in Costa Rica, Honduras, and Mexico, who now lead rainforest walks, birdwatching tours, and whalewatching and kayaking trips. On average, individual incomes have risen 92 percent as a result of this training—with most of the money going back into the local economy.[103]

Nepal's Annapurna Conservation Area Project (ACAP), launched in 1986 with support from the World Wide Fund for Nature, is another example of a successful ecotourism partnership. ACAP has trained local residents—predominantly subsistence farmers, herders, and traders—in such skills as food preparation and menu costing, safety and security for trekkers, and carpet weaving, allowing them to integrate tourism with their own farming activities and handicrafts. The project has helped conserve forests and other resources by setting up microhydroelectricity plants on streams and installing solar water heaters in the lodges, while residents manage a revolving fund to help pay for latrines and garbage pits. Though ACAP is funded mostly through foreign donations and entry fees from trekkers, villagers are encouraged to put up half of the funding in order to increase local involvement and eventually make the project self-reliant. Largely as a result of the project, tourist numbers to the region have soared from 14,300 in 1980 to more than 63,000 today.[104]

Across the developing world, growing numbers of poachers and other resource users are becoming tour guides. . . .

Growing numbers of privately owned tour operations are also supporting local initiatives by donating a portion of their profits to conservation, particularly as they recognize its value for their own survival. One German tour company that leads trips to Croatia, for instance, contributes a portion of its fee to conserving the country's rare Adriatic dolphins. And since 1997, New York-based Lindblad Expeditions has given more than $500,000 in client donations from its Galapagos trips to scientific research and environmental preservation efforts in the archipelago.[105]

Key players in the international community are also pledging support for ecotourism projects, often in alliance with local or international businesses and NGOs. Since the mid-1980s, the U.S. Agency for International Development has worked with the private sector and conservation groups in more than a dozen countries, including Costa Rica, Jamaica, Madagascar, Sri Lanka, and Thailand—providing funding for new and existing parks, recruiting and training park staff, and helping governments promote regulated investments in lodging, guide services, and other ventures. And since 1991 the Global Environment Facility, sponsored by the World Bank and the United Nations, has channeled more than $1 billion into some 400 biodiversity-related projects in the developing world, many of which have significant ecotourism components.[106]

Ecotourism's potential benefits are not always enough of an incentive to deter governments or industry leaders from finding alternative uses for valuable land, however. And some natural sites are already too damaged from agriculture, logging, and other development to have conservation or tourism appeal. Forests in Sabah, on the tip of Borneo, have become so fragmented that populations of the large mammals that attract tourists are declining. Returns are too low to dissuade officials and private companies from clearing the rainforest for oil-palm plantations. Other potential ecotourism spots—such as western and central Africa, which are rich in elephants and other wildlife—face serious obstacles that deter tourists, such as political instability and civil unrest, lack of adequate local services and infrastructure, or remoteness from airports or other attractions.[107]

In the International Year of Ecotourism, it is important that any efforts to highlight ecotourism as the solution to tourism's problems be monitored carefully. Although the World Ecotourism Summit scheduled for Quebec in May 2002 aims to be a truly comprehensive effort, allowing all stakeholders to voice their views and to exchange information about ecotourism experiences worldwide, the event is also by its very nature an opportunity for significant tourism marketing and promotion. The heavy involvement of international agencies, governments, and the private sector could distract attention from efforts to develop more low-impact, locally run ecotourism activities, particularly in areas not prepared to handle an onslaught of tourists.[108]

As ecotourism increasingly comes into its own, it is clear that one of the biggest challenges is balancing the potential benefits with the pitfalls. Depending on how it is done, ecotourism can create its share of social and environmental problems. The degree of impact ultimately reflects the level of commitment of the enterprise, the quality of guide training, and the behavior of tourists themselves.

By definition, ecotourism will always remain a niche form of travel, relevant only in the relatively few areas of the world that still possess valuable natural attractions. It can do little to address the very real environmental problems of rampant, mass tourism at more urban destinations, such as downtown Bangkok. Thus, it should be viewed as just one possible solution in a range of strategies for more sustainable tourism development.[109]

Toward a Sustainable Tourism Industry

According to the World Tourism Organization, sustainable tourism should lead to the "management of all resources in such a way that economic, social and aesthetic needs can be fulfilled while maintaining cultural integrity, essential ecological processes, biological diversity and life support systems." Interest in making tourism more sustainable has grown steadily over the past decade, particularly in the wake of the 1992 U.N. conference in Rio. Although tourism was barely mentioned in that meeting's blueprint for action, *Agenda 21*, countries have since endorsed international declarations on a wide range of related topics, including tourism and sustainable development, the social impacts of tourism, tourism and biodiversity, and tourism and ethics. (See Table 4.) In an important milestone, the World Tourism Organization, the World Travel & Tourism Council, and the Earth Council drafted their own *Agenda 21 for the Travel and*

TABLE 4

Key International Milestones in Sustainable Tourism

Year   Event

1992 **Agenda 21:** Though tourism is not a specific agenda item at the Rio
      Earth Summit, the conference report briefly mentions it in chapters on
      mountain and coastal ecosystems.

1995 **Charter on Sustainable Tourism:** Delegates at the World Conference
      on Sustainable Tourism in Canary Islands agree on 18 priority points for
      sustainable tourism development.

1996 **Agenda 21 for the Travel and Tourism Industry:** Backed by the
      World Tourism Organization, WTTC, and Earth Council, the report out-
      lines key measures that governments and the tourism industry can take
      toward sustainability.

1997 **Malé Declaration on Sustainable Tourism:** Tourism and environment
      ministers from Asia and the Pacific agree on general guidelines for the
      sustainable development of tourism.

1997 **Manila Declaration on the Social Impact of Tourism:** Governments
      and private groups from 77 countries and territories pledge to better
      involve local communities in tourism planning and to address the social
      abuses and exploitation arising from tourism.

1997 **Berlin Declaration on Biological Diversity and Sustainable
      Tourism:** Environment ministers from 18 countries pledge to recognize
      the role of ecologically sound tourism in biodiversity conservation and
      call on international banks and donors to support sustainable tourism
      projects in developing countries.

1999 **UN Commission on Sustainable Development's Working
      Programme for Sustainable Tourism:** This first action-oriented work
      program on sustainable tourism recognizes the need for sustainable
      tourism development that safeguards local culture and the environment.

1999 **World Tourism Organization's Global Code of Ethics for Tourism:**
      Sets out global rules of the game for tourism stakeholders and creates
      an overall framework for applying sustainable tourism practices.

1999 **World Bank/World Tourism Organization Alliance:** The two institu-
      tions agree to cooperate in sustainable tourism development, with the
      Bank pledging to encourage private sector development and foreign
      investment in sustainable tourism and to help governments formulate
      clear policy objectives.

Table 4 (continued)

2000 **UNEP's Principles for Implementation of Sustainable Tourism:**
A set of guidelines to help governments, industry, and other stakeholders—including UNEP conventions that address tourism issues—to apply the general concept of sustainable tourism in practice and to minimize environmental impacts from tourism.

2002 **United Nations International Year of Ecotourism:** Governments, the tourism industry, and other stakeholders will have an opportunity to review and share their experiences with ecotourism at the World Ecotourism Summit in May.

Source: See endnote 110.

Tourism Industry in 1996, outlining key steps for the industry, governments, and others.[110]

Making tourism more sustainable requires careful planning at all levels and the involvement of all people with a stake in it—including the local communities that will be directly affected by tourism's presence. At its core, however, tourism is a private sector activity, driven in large part by international hotel chains, tour companies, and other businesses. Sustainability will therefore require systemic change in the ways this industry operates. But reconciling the industry drive for more tourists with the need for sustainable practices will not necessarily be easy.[111]

Nevertheless, the tourism industry has taken many positive steps to become more environmentally and socially responsible. This change is in part a response to growing consumer pressure for more environment-friendly tourism products. A 1997 study by the Travel Industry Association of America reports that some 83 percent of the public supported green travel services, and that people were willing to spend 6 percent more on average for travel services and products provided by environmentally responsible companies. In a similar survey in the United Kingdom, more than half the interviewees said that when planning vacations or business trips, they would find it important to deal with a company that takes environmental issues into account.[112]

At the very least, industry leaders are beginning to recognize the link between responsible stewardship and financial self-interest. Perhaps more than any other industry, tourism depends on a clean environment. Declines in environmental quality can hit industry pocketbooks directly. Conversely, helping to make destinations more attractive and supporting more environmentally sensitive practices can boost the profits of tourism businesses.[113]

Many of the world's larger tourism companies, from hotels to tour operators, are taking formal steps to restructure their management and operations along environmental lines—including reducing consumption of water, energy, and other resources and improving the management, handling, and disposal of waste. Some are adopting the environmental management standard set out by the International Standards Organization, ISO 140001. In addition to saving money, these transformational moves are important to sustainability. *Agenda 21* ranks the incorporation of environmental management principles as "among the highest corporate priorities and as a key determinant to sustainability."[114]

Changes in the hotel industry can be particularly fruitful, not only because these facilities consume large quantities of resources, but also because they can have enormous influence over the broader habits and practices of their guests, employees, and suppliers. A simple step such as outfitting rooms with cards that encourage guests to reuse linens and towels when they are staying more than one night can conserve on average 114 liters (30 gallons) of water per room each day, plus energy—at a daily cost savings of at least $1.50 per room. The Texas-based Green Hotels Association has generated positive results in its efforts to spread the use of such cards in the United States: a representative from the Holiday Inn chain reported that 80 percent of guests that stayed multiple nights participated in the program.[115]

Worldwide, hotels are embracing a wide range of environmental actions, from installing solar lighting and purchasing biodegradable housekeeping supplies to composting beach seaweed for hotel gardens and loaning bicycles to guests. By implementing its environmental management program, Inter-Continental Hotels reduced overall energy costs by 27 percent between 1988 and 1995. In 1995 alone the chain saved $3.7 million, cutting its sulfur dioxide emissions by 10,670 kilograms and saving 610,866 cubic meters of water—an average water reduction of nearly 7 percent per hotel, despite higher occupancies. Other large hotel chains have made similar steps in this direction. (See Table 5.)[116]

Spearheading this movement at the global level is the London-based International Hotels Environment Initiative (IHEI), which works with hotels, hotel associations, suppliers, tourist boards, governments, and NGOs to encourage environmentally and socially responsible business practice. Founded in 1992, IHEI represents more than 8,000 hotels in 111 countries, including international chains such as Hilton, Marriott, Radisson SAS, Taj Group, Scandic, and Forte. In 1995, it joined with UNEP and the 700,000-member International Hotel and Restaurant Association to release an "Environmental Action Pack for Hotels," outlining ways for hotels to integrate environmental management principles and to reduce energy and water use, waste, and emissions.[117]

The cruise industry, too, is making an effort to integrate environmental management practices into its activities, though much remains to be done. Some companies are embracing relatively simple initiatives such as recycling plasticware and using recyclable and reusable containers. Holland America, Princess Cruises, and other lines are outfitting newer vessels with on-board water treatment plants, incinerators, or co-generation incinerators that harness energy from waste burning, though critics have raised concern about the health impacts of toxic emissions. Older vessels continue to have only limited options for waste disposal.[118]

In a significant step, in June 2001 the International Council of Cruise Lines, a powerful industry lobbying group

TABLE 5

Hotel "Greening" Success Stories

Hotel or Hotel Chain	"Greening" Initiative
Hilton International	In recent years, has saved 60 percent on gas costs and 30 percent on both electricity and water costs, while cutting wastes by 25 percent. Vienna Hilton and Vienna Plaza reduced laundry loads by164,000 kilograms per year, minimizing water and chemical use.
Singapore Marriott and Tang Plaza	Water conservation efforts save some 40,000 cubic meters of water per year—a reduction of nearly 20 percent.
Scandic	Has reduced water use by 20 percent per guest in recent years. Has also pioneered a 97 percent recyclable hotel room and is building or retrofitting 1,500 annually.
Sheraton Rittenhouse Square, Philadelphia	Boasts a 93 percent recycled granite floor, organic cotton bedding, night tables made from discarded wooden shipping pallets, naturally dyed recycled carpeting, and nontoxic wallpaper, carpeting, drapes, and cleaning products. The extra 2 percent investment more than paid for itself in the first six months.
Inter-Continental Hotels and Resorts	Hotels must implement a checklist of 134 environmental actions and meet specific energy, waste, and water management targets. Between 1988 and 1995, the chain reduced overall energy costs by 27 percent. In 1995, it saved $3.7 million, reducing sulfur dioxide emissions by 10,670 kilograms, and saved 610,866 cubic meters of water—an average water reduction of nearly 7 percent per hotel, despite higher occupancies.
Forte Brighouse, West Yorkshire, United Kingdom	A transition to energy-efficient lamps reduced energy use by 45 percent, cut maintenance by 85 percent, and lowered carbon emissions by 135 tons. The move paid for itself in savings in less than a year.
Hyatt International	In the United States, energy efficiency measures cut energy use by 15 percent and now save the chain an estimated $15 million annually.
Holiday Inn Crowne Plaza, Schiphol Airport, Netherlands	By offering guests the option of not changing their linens and towels each day, the hotel reduced laundry volume, water, and detergent, as well as costs, by 20 percent.

Source: See endnote 116.

that represents the world's 16 biggest cruise lines, adopted new mandatory waste management standards for its members. The members' 90 ships together carry more than 7 million passengers annually—over three quarters of all cruise tourists. Companies risk losing their membership if they fail to abide by the guidelines, which among other things set new rules for the disposal of wastewater, used batteries, and photo processing and dry cleaning chemicals. The guidelines also call on members to strengthen compliance with domestic and international environmental laws.[119]

There are also growing international efforts to get tour operators, their staff, and their clients to adopt more environmentally sound practices. Tour operators and travel agents can play a big part in redirecting tourism because they help determine not only where tourists go, but also which services they use. Many tour companies are setting up professional guide accreditation programs and investing in extensive training to ensure that their guides adhere to sound practices.[120]

In March 2000, UNEP, in cooperation with UNESCO and the World Tourism Organization, launched a voluntary Tour Operator's Initiative, calling on members to share and implement best practices and to integrate sustainability concerns into their operational management and tour design. The effectiveness of the initiative remains to be seen, however. Of the 20 companies that have signed on—including British Airways Holidays, Thomas Cook Ltd., Germany's ITS Reisen, and groups in India, Italy, Japan, Morocco, Sweden, Thailand, Turkey, and the United States—many demonstrated a strong environmental commitment before participating in the group, which suggests that the initiative may be preaching to the converted. For instance, British Airways Holidays, with offices in some 77 countries, was one of the first major tour operators to adopt a policy and action program for the environment, in 1993.[121]

Moreover, many high-level sustainability efforts fail to reach the less elaborate tour operations, accommodations, and services that most of the world's tourists use. Indeed, a survey in Australia's Gold Coast region found that while energy and water conservation measures were as common in three- and four-star hotels as in five-star ones, they were rarely adopted in one- or two-star accommodations. To be effective, particularly in the developing world, environmental management must be implemented at these levels as well.[122]

One way to push the wider adoption of sustainable practices is to accelerate the transfer of environmentally sound technologies, practices, and management tools. For instance, donors, banks, and businesses in industrial countries could support desalination plants and other water-saving systems, renewable energy technologies, and the adoption of ecologically sound chemical management. Banks and insurance companies could incorporate environmental and social criteria into assessment procedures for loans, investments, and insurance. Companies could use environmental impact reviews or green auditing measures to monitor progress.[123]

In addition to structural changes in management and operations, tourism businesses of all sizes and types are embracing a wide range of less formal voluntary initiatives to regulate their impacts, with mixed success. Forty-six of Antarctica's main tour operators, for instance, now belong to the International Association of Antarctic Tour Operators, a voluntary body formed in 1991 that has developed a strict code of conduct for tour operators and their clients. But despite regulations that include landing no more than 100 people per site at a time and making sure visitors do not disturb wildlife, tourists still pick up penguins, approach seals, and drive birds from their nests.[124]

Tourism businesses are also participating in voluntary certification schemes that grant a seal of approval to companies or destinations that demonstrate environmentally or socially sound practice. Europe's Blue Flag Campaign, for instance, awards a yearly "eco-label" to beaches and marinas that maintain high environmental standards and sanitary and safe facilities. (See Table 6.) Not only do these labels serve as useful marketing tools, but they can also spur the tourism industry to develop more environmentally friendly products. Moreover, they can provide consumers with valuable information about the range of sustainable tourism products, helping them to make more informed travel choices.[125]

Unfortunately, more than 100 competing tourism certification schemes exist worldwide, and there are as yet no international guidelines to help travelers evaluate them. Though many of these schemes are developed in partnership with government agencies or NGOs that independently issue or monitor the certification standards, others are based on self-evaluation or paid membership, which may simply allow companies to "buy" their way to a green label. Ultimately, the success of tourism certification will depend on whether it can set a trusted, reliable standard, and on the degree to which the industry and consumers embrace it worldwide.[126]

It is too soon to tell whether industry voluntary initiatives are making a real difference on the ground, or if they are largely "greenwashing" tools used to create the perception of environmental concern. The industry-sponsored *Agenda 21 for the Travel and Tourism Industry*, for instance, places significant emphasis on these forms of self-regulation, while continuing to uphold the dominant role of open and competitive markets, privatization, and deregulation in spurring tourism's growth. It makes little mention of direct government regulation or international instruments such as tourism taxes.[127]

Moreover, while many industry efforts embrace a shift toward environmental sustainability, they are less willing to incorporate social and cultural needs, such as addressing labor and employment issues, protecting cultures, and maximizing linkages with local economies and communities. One tourism company that has been more successful at this than most is Conservation Corporation Africa, a hotel management group based in South Africa that employs and trains more than 2,500 people across the region and offers small-scale loans to help local residents start their own businesses.[128]

TABLE 6

Selected Tourism Certification Efforts Worldwide

Green Globe 21 – Has awarded logos to some 500 companies and destinations in more than 100 countries.

Rewards efforts to incorporate social responsibility and *Agenda 21* principles into business programs. But may confuse tourists by rewarding not only businesses that have achieved certification, but also those that have simply committed to undertake the process.

ECOTEL® – Has certified 23 hotels in Latin America, seven in the United States and Mexico, five in Japan, and one in India.

Assigns hotels zero to five globes based on environmental commitment, waste management, energy efficiency, water conservation, environmental education, and community involvement. Hotels must be reinspected every two years, and unannounced inspections can occur at anytime. A project of the industry consulting group HVS International.

European Blue Flag Campaign – Includes more than 2,750 sites in 21 European countries; being adopted in South Africa and the Caribbean.

Awards a yearly ecolabel to beaches and marinas for their high environmental standards and sanitary and safe facilities. Credited with improving the quality and desirability of European coastal sites. Run by the international nonprofit Foundation for Environmental Education.

Certification for Sustainable Tourism, Costa Rica – Has certified some 54 hotels since 1997.

Gives hotels a ranking of one to five based on environmental and social criteria. Credited with raising environmental awareness among tourism businesses and tourists. But the rating is skewed toward large hotels that may be too big to really be sustainable.

SmartVoyager, Galapagos, Ecuador – Since 1999, has certified five of more than 80 ships that operate in the area.

Gives a special seal to tour operators and boats that voluntarily comply with specified benchmarks for boat and dinghy maintenance and operation, dock operations, and management of wastewater and fuels. A joint project of the Rainforest Alliance and a local conservation group.

Green Leaf, Thailand – Had certified 59 hotels as of October 2000.

Awards hotels between one and five "green leaves" based on audits of their environmental policies and other measures. Aims to improve efficiency and raise awareness within the domestic hotel industry.

Source: See endnote 125.

Beyond the Industry: Other Supporting Players

As the changing rules of the global economy further open markets to tourism development, governments, international institutions, NGOs, and tourists themselves will need to play a proactive role in getting sustainable tourism on track. But this will not be easy. Tourism's rapid growth has been facilitated in large part by an absence of outside interference; like most industries, the tourism industry opposes intervention that it perceives as damaging to competitiveness and profits. And all signs indicate that instead of tightening regulations, governments are granting greater leeway to private interests.[129]

One way governments can help move tourism in a better direction is by developing regulatory and policy frameworks that support key environmental and social goals, without stifling incentives for investment. Planning authorities at the national, regional, and local levels can work to better integrate tourism into overall strategies for sustainable development. Australia's 1992 National Ecotourism Strategy, which recognizes the need for "responsible tourism planning and management to protect the country's natural and cultural heritage," is a good model. Similarly, a 1997 recommendation by the Council of Europe calls on member governments to limit tourism development to a level compatible with ecological and social carrying capacity, including supporting activities that benefit local communities and controlling construction along coastlines. Both Costa Rica and Belize have national policies or strategies to promote ecotourism.[130]

Many countries still do not have broad plans, however. And those that do typically fail to address social or environmental sustainability. Viet Nam's Tourism Master Plan, for instance, aims to attract large-scale investment primarily through joint ventures between foreign corporations and state enterprises, but it does little to support small-scale entrepreneurs or protect ethnic minorities from exploitation by external operators. In general, because tourism activities cut across a variety of government departments and industry groups, it is often difficult for authorities to coordinate a unified plan of action for addressing the impacts.[131]

To ensure greater benefits for local communities and the environment, national and local governments will need to balance large-scale investments in hotels, restaurants, and other facilities with smaller-scale initiatives that are actively planned and managed by local communities, such as family-run lodges or informal craft cooperatives. Though homegrown enterprises alone cannot accommodate growing tourism numbers or generate the same levels of revenue and employment as larger investments, they can expand opportunities for poor and indigenous groups and ensure that tourism's profits are spread more widely.[132]

Local participation not only brings residents greater job satisfaction, it also gives them greater responsibility for an initiative's outcome and encourages them to take a longer-term view toward conserving their local environment and resources. At the same time, smaller-scale tourism growth tends to be slower and more controlled, and can help offset tourism's negative environmental and cultural impacts by allowing more gradual integration of new activities into communities. Many countries, including Brazil, Indonesia, Namibia, and Nepal, are incorporating small-scale, community-based initiatives into national tourism efforts.[133]

To help get more responsible tourism off the ground, governments will need policies, regulations, and programs that boost local land and resource ownership, facilitate market access, and sanction exploitative businesses. Tourism agencies and other local government bodies can provide low-cost licensing to residents as well as training in languages, small business development, and marketing, and can offer incentives like tax breaks, special interest rates, or microenterprise loans. These types of support are desperately needed: in South Africa, where the government is hoping to achieve 60 percent black ownership of the travel industry within five years, tour operations still remain largely white-owned, in part because few black South Africans possess the capital or relevant experience.[134]

Government agencies that oversee and approve tourism planning can also act as intermediaries between externally owned tourism companies and the interests of local residents. They can encourage these businesses to re-invest their profits at the destination, for instance by supporting local agriculture and construction, funding area conservation efforts, and training and hiring local staff, including women. To minimize tourism's negative impacts on employment, governments can set labor standards and place restrictions on exploitative businesses such as sex tourism or child labor. A new law in Nepal, for example, prohibits children under the age of 14 from working in trekking, rafting, casinos and other tourism-related jobs, though critics charge that enforcement is weak.[135]

National and regional land use planning that considers the diverse needs of local residents, tourists, and other users, as well as of the environment, is an important element of a sustainable tourism strategy. It gives tourism authorities greater say over whether development occurs in an environmentally or culturally sensitive area and in a controlled manner. A new government plan in Spain's Balearic Islands, for example, oversees the careful zoning of certain areas for facilities like hotels, green areas, sanitary services, and parking. In Denmark, Egypt, France, and Spain, laws forbid developers from building within a specified distance from the coast in order to prevent beach erosion. And at Cuba's Cayo Coco, where hotels must have no more than four stories and are required to be set back from the beach, each new building must go through an extensive government environmental impact assessment before construction is approved.[136]

One country that has been successful in its efforts to integrate social and environmental variables into land use planning is Namibia. Under a bold government plan developed in the early 1990s, local communities can assume legal responsibility for zoning their own agriculture, wildlife, and tourism activities in multi-use areas known as conservancies, and then derive direct financial benefits from them. Thirteen communities had registered conservancies as of early 2001, while another 20–24 were under development—bringing large tracts of the country under local tourism management. A national association for community-based tourism, started in 1995, provides advice and training to these communities and helps them to market their lodges and other ventures at international travel fairs and other promotional events.[137]

Elsewhere, governments are mitigating tourism's impacts by restricting the actual number of visitors allowed at a natural area or cultural site—though determining the appropriate level of use is often difficult. The Peruvian government recently decreed that no more than 500 people a day can hike to Machu Picchu (down from as many as 1,000), in addition to more than tripling the fee and requiring tourists to trek with a registered company. On a larger scale, the Himalayan kingdom of Bhutan practices an official policy of "high-value, low-volume" tourism and accepted only 7,500 visitors in all of the year 2000, at a cost of $250 each per day. Elsewhere, natural areas are being roped off completely: visitors to Ecuador's Galapagos Islands are restricted to only 18 sites, while the country's Pasachoa Park closes for a full month each year to allow for environmental restoration.[138]

One alternative to barring visitors is to try to limit the impact of those who do come. In Nepal, several local governments have banned the use of plastic bags or containers in their region in an effort to reduce pollution and litter. And visitors to the country's remote Upper Mustang region are required to take precautions like bringing their own kerosene for fuel to prevent deforestation, disposing of waste properly or carrying it with them, and not giving money or goods to local children. Other tourist sites worldwide are designating special trails that lead visitors away from sensitive areas to protect them from excessive damage.[139]

In addition to regulations, governments are using economic instruments to encourage responsible tourism. These include charging user fees, offering grants that reward "good practice" in tourism, and levying eco-taxes on everything from accommodation to air and marine transport. In 1995, for example, France adopted a tax on marine public transport to several protected islands to raise additional funds for their management and protection. And to offset the environmental impact of flights, one small London airport is asking travelers to pay a voluntary fee of up to $4.24, which would be used to plant carbon-absorbing trees. By more accurately pricing tourism services to reflect their toll on the environment, governments can push tourists and the industry to pay a fairer share in maintaining tourism assets.[140]

Many countries are incorporating small-scale, community-based initiatives into national tourism efforts.

Yet such levies are often highly controversial because businesses fear they will deter tourists. Local enterprises in Spain's Balearic Islands, for example, are fighting the regional government's April 2001 decision to charge tourists up to $1.78 extra per night at accommodations, even though the fee would pay for improving tourist areas and managing natural spaces to protect them against environmental damage. A similar effort by the Indian Ocean island of Seychelles to introduce a $90 eco-tax on all foreign visitors fell through in 1998. And a proposed $50 per head passenger tax on Caribbean cruises was reportedly dropped in the early 1990s after complaints from U.S. cruise lines. Indeed, rather than levying taxes, many governments instead offer tax holidays, loans, and other incentives to attract tourism investors.[141]

Governments can take action at the international level by supporting the implementation of regional and global environmental treaties, such as the climate change and biodiversity conventions. But efforts to address tourism explicitly in some of these treaties have met strong resistance. For instance, many small island states and some European countries oppose the establishment of global guidelines on ecotourism under the Convention on Biological Diversity out of concern that governments and the industry would perceive ecotourism primarily as a new market opportunity, and that the rules would accelerate the privatization of biodiversity worldwide. Governments can also work to ensure that international trade agreements like GATS and TRIMS do not undermine domestic environmental and labor regulations or compromise broader development goals.[142]

Currently, many developing-country governments lack the capacity or will to take on a greater oversight or regulatory role. Fiscal and planning instruments are often too weak to influence the direction of tourism investments effectively, while local authorities may have only limited enforcement power. Many governments are relying on outside groups for additional support. International lending institutions like the World Bank and the Asian Development Bank (ADB), for instance, have stepped up their funding for sustainable tourism and related infrastructure improvements. In 2001, the ADB approved a $2.2 million loan to improve solid waste infrastructure and management in the Cook Islands. In addition to funding large-scale investments and environmental improvements, regional lending institutions as well as the World Bank could also earmark greater support for smaller-scale enterprises.[143]

Other international institutions are working to create benchmarks for sustainable tourism that will make it easier for governments and businesses to measure progress. The World Tourism Organization has tested nine core indicators to assess the health of tourist destinations, based on environmental factors such as levels of use, development, protection, and waste management, as well as social variables like tourist and resident satisfaction. The organization has also developed a hotel audit program to help owners of smaller hotels become more environmentally responsible. And the International Maritime Organization oversees and enforces international labor and environmental standards on shipping and other maritime activities, including those affecting cruise ships.[144]

There are also efforts to publicize instances where

progress toward sustainable tourism is being made. UNEP, in cooperation with the World Tourism Organization, UNESCO, and industry associations, publishes technical reports on best practices in the tourism industry and organizes conferences and workshops to help governments, the private sector, and other groups share experiences and become more sustainable.[145]

Over the past few decades, nongovernmental players — including citizen groups, grassroots activists, and tourists themselves—have generated much of the pressure for more sustainable tourism. Local involvement can spell the difference between positive and negative tourism developments. "Destinations often attract the tourists they deserve," says Robyn Bushell, professor of tourism at the University of Western Sydney. "If locals aren't proud and active, and businesses aren't required by local governments to value a place, then nor will the visitors."[146]

Notably, it is a citizens' coalition, and not the government or the industry, which is finally taking the initiative to deal with the waste problems at India's Kovalam beach. In February 2001, activists with a local environmental group (Thanal), aided by Greenpeace India, launched Zero Waste Kovalam—a project that aims to convert the village into a zero-waste community by incorporating strategies of reduction, recycling, and reuse into the various waste streams. If the initiative wins industry and government backing, it may become a model for similar efforts across India.[147]

Communities and international activist groups are having similar success combating unsustainable tourism developments elsewhere, but this remains an uphill battle. In April 2001, these groups played a big role in convincing the Mexican government to revoke permits for five hotel companies to build resorts, golf courses, and other facilities at X'cacel, a 165-hectare stretch of beach south of Cancun that is home to 40 protected species and a key nesting site for endangered sea turtles. And the U.K.-based lobbying group Tourism Concern has successfully persuaded many tour operators to stop advertising Myanmar (formerly Burma) as a destination in protest against that country's human rights violations.[148]

Tourists themselves have a growing responsibility to understand the environmental and social impacts of their travel. Industry groups and NGOs can help promote more sustainable behavior through public awareness campaigns and tourist training. These groups can inform consumers by providing brochures or guidelines at travel agencies or including awareness materials with the health and safety information that is already distributed for many countries. Tourism Concern, for example, has produced five in-flight videos warning tourists about the crime of child sex tourism, and the World Travel & Tourism Council has created a video series on tourism's environmental impact aimed at airlines and schools. The relatively low visibility of these initiatives, however, suggests that much remains to be done to boost tourist education.[149]

Before departing on trips, travelers can research whether the companies they are supporting are environmentally and culturally sensitive, hire local staff, or give a portion of their profits to local communities or conservation efforts. The International Ecotourism Society's "Your Travel Choice Makes a Difference" campaign helps travelers choose responsible tour operators and guides and offers "green" travel advice on their website. Groups like Conservation International and Responsible Travel also selectively advertise eco-friendly trips over the Internet.[150]

Once at their destinations, tourists can choose to follow visitor rules and regulations, buy local food and crafts, not purchase souvenirs made from endangered animals, and stay in lower-impact lodging, though in the absence of audits and standards, the degree of impact can be difficult to determine. They can minimize cultural disruption by thinking of themselves as guests: learning about local customs and language, asking before taking a photograph or entering sacred spaces, supporting local performers or craftspeople, and generally respecting the rights of others.[151]

Ultimately, sustainable tourism means traveling with

an awareness of our larger impact on Earth. This is something for everyone to keep in mind—from governments promoting tourism, to tourism businesses and tourists themselves. Together, these groups can balance the ultimate goal of satisfying tourist demand with key environmental and social objectives, both minimizing tourism's impacts and boosting its benefits.

Appendix: Tourism Links

International Organizations

World Tourism Organization
Capitán Haya 42,28020 Madrid, Spain
tel.: 34 91 567 81 00; fax 34 91 571 37 33
e-mail: omt@world-tourism.org; website: www.world-tourism.org
Collects data on tourism and helps governments and organizations translate environmental concerns into practical policies and measures.

UNEP Division of Technology, Industry, and Economics: Tourism
39-43, Quai André Citroën, 75739 Paris Cedex 15, France
tel.: 33 1 44 37 14 41; fax: 33 1 44 37 14 74
e-mail: unep.tie@unep.fr; website: www.uneptie.org/tourism
Helps governments, NGOs, businesses, and other organizations implement sustainable tourism through demonstration projects, training activities, and support for voluntary initiatives.

UNEP Tour Operator's Initiative
39-43, Quai André Citroën, 75739 Paris Cedex 15, France
tel.: 33 1 44 37 14 50; fax: 33 1 44 37 14 74
e-mail: unep.tie@unep.fr; website: www.toinitiative.org
Works with tour operators of all sizes to promote and disseminate methods and practices compatible with sustainable tourism development.

Industry Links

World Travel & Tourism Council
1-2 Queen Victoria Terrace, Sovereign Court
London E1W 3HA, United Kingdom
tel.: 44 870 727 9882 ; fax: 44 870 728 9882
e-mail: enquiries@wttc.org; website: www.wttc.org
Collects data on tourism, and works with industry members to raise awareness of sustainable tourism and promote best practices.

International Hotels Environment Initiative
The Prince of Wales International Business Leaders Forum (IBLF)
15-16 Cornwall Terrace, Regent's Park
London NW1 4QP, United Kingdom
tel.: 44 20 7467 3600; fax: 44 20 7467 3610
e-mail: info@iblf.org; website: www.ihei.org

Provides practical guidance to the global hotel industry, tour operators, and their suppliers on how to improve environmental performance.

Green Hotels Association
P. O. Box 420212
Houston, TX 77242-0212 USA
tel.: (713) 789-8889; fax (713) 789-9786
e-mail: green@greenhotels.com; www.greenhotels.com
Offers practical suggestions, ideas, and products to promote and support the "greening" of the lodging industry.

Business Enterprises for Sustainable Travel
The Conference Board
845 Third Avenue
New York, NY 0022-6678 USA
tel.: (212) 759-0900; website: www.sustainabletravel.org
Works to encourage the adoption of sustainable practices within the travel and tourism industry by providing examples of best practice and supporting community pilot projects.

International Council of Cruise Lines
2111 Wilson Boulevard, 8th floor
Arlington, VA 22201 USA
tel.: (800) 595-9338; fax: (703) 522-3811
e-mail: info@iccl.org; website: www.iccl.org
Helps the cruise industry incorporate comprehensive waste management programs into its operations and sets environmental and other standards for member vessels.

International Association of Antarctic Tour Operators
P.O. Box 2178
Basalt, CO 81621 USA
tel.: (970) 704-1047; fax: (970) 704-9660
e-mail: iaato@iaato.org; website: www.iaato.org
Works to advocate, promote, and practice safe and environmentally responsible travel to the Antarctic.

Ecotourism Links

The International Ecotourism Society
P.O. Box 668
Burlington, VT 05402 USA
tel.: (802) 651-9818; fax: (802) 651-9819
e-mail: ecomail@ecotourism.org; website: www.ecotourism.org
Disseminates a wide range of information about ecotourism.

Ecotravel Center
Conservation International
1919 M Street, NW, Suite 600
Washington, DC 20036 USA
tel.: (202) 912-1000, or toll-free (within the U.S.) (800) 406-2306
website: www.ecotour.org
Provides information about travel opportunities that benefit conservation and local communities around the world.

Planeta.com
Mexico City, Mexico
e-mail: ron@planeta.com; website: www.planeta.com
Provides practical tips and in-depth scholarly reports about ecotourism and hosts a variety of online forums and conferences.

RARE Center for Tropical Conservation
1840 Wilson Boulevard, Suite 402
Arlington, VA 22201-3000 USA
tel.: (703) 522-5070; fax: (703) 522-5027
e-mail: rare@rarecenter.org; website: www.rarecenter.org
Works with local communities, NGO's, and others to raise awareness about biodiversity and to get local people involved in protecting their natural resources, primarily through ecotourism.

Big Volcano Ecotourism Resource Center
website: www.bigvolcano.com.au/ercentre/ercpage.htm
Offers comprehensive information on ecotourism, general tourism, and best practices in travel worldwide.

Centre for Environmentally Responsible Tourism
United Kingdom
e-mail: info@cert.org; website: www.c-e-r-t.org
Highlights tour operators that have environmental policies in place and are supporting and developing sustainable tourism.

Partners in Responsible Tourism
P.O. Box 237
San Francisco, CA 94104-0237
tel.: (415) 675-0420
e-mail: info@pirt.org; website: www.pirt.org
A network of individuals and representatives of tourism companies who have a strong interest in adventure travel and ecotourism.

Responsible Travel
e-mail: info@responsibletravel.com
website: www.responsibletravel.com
Offers an extensive selection of responsible/eco-travel trips and
accommodations.

Additional Links

Tourism Concern
Stapleton House, 277-281 Holloway Road
London N7 8HN, United Kingdom
tel.: 44 20 7753 3330; fax: 44 20 7753 3331
e-mail: info@tourismconcern.org.uk
website: www.tourismconcern.org.uk
Works to raise awareness of tourism's impacts among government
decision-makers, the tourist industry, tourism activists, students,
and the general public.

Pro-Poor Tourism Project
e-mail: ppt@odi.org.uk; website: www.propoortourism.org.uk
Conducts and publishes case studies on tourism initiatives that
generate net benefits for the world's poor. Offers practical suggestions on how the tourism industry, governments, and communities can support "pro-poor" tourism initiatives.

Rethinking Tourism Project
366 North Prior Avenue, Suite 203
St. Paul, MN 55104 USA
tel.: (651) 644-9984; fax: (651) 644-2720
e-mail: info@rethinkingtourism.org
website: www.rethinkingtourism.org
Provides information and resources about tourism and its impacts on
indigenous peoples and cultures and facilitates indigenous participation
in related policymaking forums, conferences, and workshops.

Bluewater Network
300 Broadway, Suite 28
San Francisco, CA 94133 USA
tel.: (415) 788-3666; fax: (415) 788-7324
e-mail: bluewater@earthisland.org
website: www.bluewaternetwork.org
Campaigns to raise awareness of and fight environmental abuse
among the shipping, oil, and motorized recreation industries,
including the cruise industry.

Green Globe 21
7 St Stephens Court, St Stephens Road,
Bournemouth BH2 6LA, United Kingdom
tel.: 44 1202 312001; fax: 44 1202 312002
e-mail: info@greenglobe21.com; website: www.greenglobe.org
Seeks to raise industry awareness of the benefits of sound environmental practice and certifies tourism companies that have taken specific steps to improve their environmental performance.

Blue Flag Campaign
The Danish Outdoor Council
Scandiagade 13, DK - 2450 Copenhagen SV
Denmark
tel.: 45 33 79 00 79; fax: 45 33 79 01 79
e-mail: bf.int@friluftsraadet.dk; website: www.blueflag.org
Provides benchmarks for sound environmental practice and grants a seal of approval to beaches and marinas that adhere to strict environmental and safety standards.

Notes

1. Jayakumar Chelaton, Thanal Conservation Action and Information Network, Kerala, India, e-mail to author, 9 July 2001.

2. Ibid.

3. Ibid.

4. International tourist arrivals refers to the number of non-residents arriving who stay at least one night. Estimates for 2000 from World Travel & Tourism Council (WTTC), "Tourism Satellite Accounting Confirms Travel and Tourism as World's Foremost Economic Activity," press release (London: 11 May 2000); arrivals numbers from Rosa Songel, Statistics and Economic Measurement of Tourism, World Tourism Organization (WTO), e-mail to author, 17 April 2001; effects of terrorism from WTO, "Tourism Knocked Down, But Not Out," press release (Madrid: 17 September 2001).

5. Songel, op. cit. note 4; one in five from Martha Honey, *Ecotourism and Sustainable Development: Who Owns Paradise?* (Washington, DC: Island Press, 1999), p. 8.

6. U.N. Conference on Trade and Development (UNCTAD), "Tourism and Development in the Least Developed Countries," background paper for the Third U.N. Conference on the Least Developed Countries, Las Palmas, Canary Islands, 26–29 March 2001; Susan C. Stonich, "Political Ecology of Tourism," *Annals of Tourism Research*, vol. 25, no. 1 (1998), p. 25.

7. Surplus from World Trade Organization, Council for Trade in Services, "Tourism Services," background note (Geneva: 23 September 1998), p. 3; 10 percent from Henryk Handszuh, "Overview of International Trade in Tourism Services, Including Current Statistics and Trends," presentation at WTO Symposium on Tourism Services, Geneva, 22–23 February 2001; 40 percent derived from World Bank, *World Development Indicators*, electronic database, accessed 6 August 2001, and from WTO, *Tourism Market Trends: World Overview and Tourism Topics* (Madrid: 2001), pp. 91–96; jobs from WTTC, "Tourism Satellite Accounting Confirms Travel and Tourism as World's Foremost Economic Activity, op. cit. note 4, and from WTTC, *Travel & Tourism's Economic Impact* (London: March 1999).

8. Deloitte & Touche, International Institute for Environment and Development (IIED), and Overseas Development Institute (ODI), *Sustainable Tourism and Poverty Elimination Study*, a report to the U.K. Department for International Development (UKDFID) (London: April 1999); least regulated from World Trade Organization, op. cit. note 7.

9. World Wide Fund for Nature (WWF International), *Preliminary Assessment of the Environmental & Social Effects of Trade in Tourism* (Gland, Switzerland: May 2001); leakage a WTO estimate cited in David Diaz

Benavides, UNCTAD, *The Sustainability of International Tourism in Developing Countries*, paper presented at the Seminar on Tourism Policy and Economic Growth, Berlin, 6–7 March 2001, pp. 8–9.

10. Caroline Ashley, Charlotte Boyd, and Harold Goodwin, "Pro-Poor Tourism: Putting Poverty at the Heart of the Tourism Agenda," *Natural Resource Perspectives* (London: ODI, March 2000).

11. United Nations Environment Programme (UNEP), "Tourism and Environmental Protection," Addendum C, Contribution of UNEP to the Secretary-General's Report on Industry and Sustainable Tourism for the Seventh Session of the UN Commission on Sustainable Development (UNCSD), New York, 1999.

12. Honey, op. cit. note 5.

13. Dieter Brand, "Sustainable Tourism—Illusion or Realistic Alternative?" *D+C*, May 2000, p. 3.

14. Joe Robinson, "Real Travel," *Utne Reader*, July–August 2001, p. 66; Mike Edwards, "The Adventures of Marco Polo, Part I," *National Geographic*, May 2001, pp. 2–31; Deborah Ramer McLaren, "The History of Indigenous Peoples and Tourism," *Cultural Survival*, summer 1999, p. 27; Bas Amelung, Pim Martens, Jan Rotmans, and Dale S. Rothman, "Tourism in Motion: Is the Sky the Limit?" in Pim Martens and Jan Rotmans, eds., *Transitions in a Globalising World* (Maastricht: International Centre for Integrative Studies, forthcoming), p. 86.

15. Robinson, op. cit. note 14; Honey, op. cit. note 5, p. 8; Roy Malkin, "The Pioneers," *UNESCO Courier*, July–August 1999, pp. 24–25.

16. Malkin, op. cit. note 15; Honey, op. cit. note 5, p. 8; Amelung et al., op. cit. note 14, p. 86; McLaren, op. cit. note 14, p. 27.

17. McLaren, op. cit. note 14, p. 29; Auliana Poon, "The 'New Tourism' Revolution," *Tourism Management*, vol. 15, no. 2 (1994), pp. 91–92; World Trade Organization, op. cit. note 7, p. 5.

18. Definitions and 2020 from World Trade Organization, op. cit. note 7, pp. 14, 47; Figure 1 from Songel, op. cit. note 4; 4–10 times higher estimate from Geoffrey Wall, Associate Dean, Graduate Studies and Research, Faculty of Environmental Studies, University of Waterloo, ON, Canada, e-mail to author, 27 September 2001.

19. Technology from World Trade Organization, op. cit. note 7, p. 6; Travel Industry Association of America, "TIA Releases Two Studies on E-Travel Consumers," press release (Washington, DC: 27 February 2001).

20. Sources of tourists from WTO, op. cit. note 7, p. 33; share of passports

derived from U.S. Department of State, conversation with Uta Saoshiro, Worldwatch Institute, 9 October 2001, and from Population Reference Bureau, electronic database, <www.prb.org/Content/NavigationMenu/Other_reports/2000-2002/sheet1.html>, viewed 9 October 2001; 3.5 and 7 percent from WTO, *Tourism 2020 Vision: A New Forecast* (Madrid: June 1998).

21. Motivations from WTO, op. cit. note 7, p. 23; Poon, op. cit. note 17; U.S. study from Honey, op. cit. note 5, p. 9.

22. Regional breakdown and Figure 2 from WTO, op. cit. note 7, p. 35, and from Songel, op. cit. note 4.

23. Asia share from WTO, op. cit. note 7, p. 35 and from Songel, op. cit. note 4; reasons for growth from World Trade Organization, op. cit. note 7, p. 5, and from David J. de Villiers, "Asia and the Pacific Tourism Trends," presentation at the 34th Annual Meeting of the Board of Governors of the Asian Development Bank, Honolulu, Hawaii, 8–11 May 2001; 2020 from WTO, op. cit. note 20, pp. 4, 11. Table 1 from WTO, op. cit. note 7, and from WTO, op. cit. note 20.

24. Receipts estimates exclude international transport fares and were deflated using U.S. Implicit GNP Price Deflator, obtained from Virginia Mannering, U.S. Commerce Department, Bureau of Economic Analysis, 27 February 2001; data and Figure 3 from WTO, op. cit. note 7, pp. 15, 17, 34, 42, and from Songel, op. cit. note 4; four times from Francesco Frangialli, "The Biggest Industry the World Has Ever Seen," *D&C*, May 2000, p. 9.

25. Data and Table 2 from WTO, op. cit. note 7, pp. 17, 34.

26. Rapid rise from WWF International, op. cit. note 9, p. 22; 8 percent and 40 percent from Handszuh, op. cit. note 7; top five from WTO, op. cit. note 7, p. 41.

27. Methodology from WTTC, *World Travel & Tourism Council Year 2001 Tourism Satellite Accounting Research: Documentation* (London: June 2001), p. 5; 2000 estimates from WTTC, op. cit. note 4.

28. Estimate of 90 percent from U.N. Environment and Development–UK (UNED–UK), *Sustainable Tourism and Poverty Elimination*, report on a workshop held 9 February 1999 in preparation for the Seventh Meeting of the U.N. Commission on Sustainable Development (UNCSD), New York, April 1999, p. 8; mergers and acquisitions and airlines from Miguel Alejandro Figueras, Advisor to the Minister of Tourism, Cuba, "International Tourism in the Cuban Economy," presentation at WTO Symposium on Tourism Services, Geneva, 22–23 February 2001, p. 7; hotels and tour operators from WTO, op. cit. note 7, p. 40.

29. World Trade Organization, op. cit. note 7, p. 7; WWF International, op. cit. note 9.

30. One in five from Honey, op. cit. note 5, p. 8; Asian destinations and growth rates from WTO, op. cit. note 7, pp. 18–22, 46; Cuba from Figueras, op. cit. note 28, p. 2.

31. UNCTAD, op. cit. note 6, p. 15.

32. World Bank from WTO, "Tourism Gaining Prestige as Development Tool," press release (Madrid: 25 June 1998) and from "World Bank Revisits Role of Tourism in Development," *World Bank News*, 18 June 1998; $500 million from Maurice Desthuis-Francis, "Tourists & Cities: Friend or Foe?" *Impact* (International Finance Corporation newsletter), spring–summer 2000, pp. 17–19; International Monetary Fund (IMF) from Raymond de Chavez, "Globalization and Tourism: Deadly Mix for Indigenous Peoples," *Third World Resurgence*, March 1999.

33. Deloitte & Touche, IIED, and ODI, op. cit. note 8, pp. 9–10; national economy estimates and Table 3 derived from World Bank, op. cit. note 7, and from WTO, op. cit. note 7, pp. 91–96.

34. UNCTAD, op. cit. note 6, pp. 3–4, 18.

35. Surplus from World Trade Organization, op. cit. note 7, p. 3; 1999 estimates from Handszuh, op. cit. note 7.

36. World Trade Organization, op. cit. note 7, pp. 7–8, 13–14; Brazil from "Wish Your Dollars Were Here," *The Economist*, 16 December 2000, p. 66.

37. Obstacles to development from UNCTAD, op. cit. note 6, pp. 9–13.

38. Deloitte and Touche, IIED, and ODI, op. cit. note 8, p. 10.

39. Sheryl Spivack, Associate Professor of Tourism Studies, George Washington University, Washington, DC, discussion with Uta Saoshiro, Worldwatch Institute, 24 October 2001.

40. Benavides, op. cit. note 9, pp. 8–9.

41. Estimates of 50–70 percent from World Trade Organization, op. cit. note 7, p. 4; linkage problems from Matthew J. Walpole and Harold J. Goodwin, "Local Economic Impacts of Dragon Tourism in Indonesia," *Annals of Tourism Research*, vol. 27, no. 3 (2000), p. 572.

42. WWF International, op. cit. note 9; Thailand from Michael Doyle, "New Law Retains US Advantage for Now," *Bangkok Post*, 8 January 2000, and from Chatrudee Theparat, "Petition Will Demand Amendment of Laws," *Bangkok Post*, 12 November 2000; crowding out from International

Labour Organisation (ILO), *Human Resources Development, Employment and Globalization in the Hotel, Catering and Tourism Sector,* report for discussion at the Tripartite Meeting on Human Resources Development, Employment and Globalization in the Hotel, Catering and Tourism Sector, Geneva, 2001, pp. 43–44.

43. Foreign operators from WWF International, op. cit. note 9, p. 15; 80 percent from Erlet Cater, "Ecotourism in the Third World: Problems for Sustainable Tourism Development," *Tourism Management,* April 1993, p. 86; packages from Ashley, Boyd, and Goodwin, op. cit. note 10.

44. Estimate of 65 percent from Polly Pattullo, *Last Resorts: The Cost of Tourism in the Caribbean* (London: Cassell, 1996), pp. 121–23; 90 percent and inflation from Cater, op. cit. note 43, p. 86.

45. Dominica from Pattullo, op. cit. note 44, pp. 121–23, and from Carlos Castilho and Roberto Herrscher, *Ecotourism: Paradise Gained, or Paradise Lost?* Panos Media Briefing No. 14 (London: Panos Institute, January 1995); Yves Renard, *Practical Strategies for Pro-Poor Tourism: A Case Study of the St. Lucia Heritage Tourism Programme,* PPT Working Paper No. 7 (London: Centre for Responsible Tourism, IIED, and ODI: April 2001).

46. David L Edgell, Sr., "A Barrier-Free Future for Tourism?" *Tourism Management,* vol. 16, no. 2 (1995), pp. 107–10; de Chavez, op. cit. note 32; WWF International, op. cit. note 9, pp. 10–11; 112 from World Trade Organization, op. cit. note 7, p. 9; TRIMS from Anita Pleumarom, "Tourism, Globalization and Sustainable Development," *Third World Resurgence,* March 1999.

47. WTTC, *Travel & Tourism's Economic Impact,* op. cit. note 7; Japan from WWF International, op. cit. note 9, p. 24.

48. Estimate of 1–2 jobs from World Bank, "World Bank Group and World Tourism Organization Examine Role of Tourism in Development," press release (Washington, DC: 25 June 1998); informal work from Ashley, Boyd, and Goodwin, op. cit. note 10. Box 1 compiled from the following sources: Carmen Michard et al., "Women's Employment in Tourism World-Wide: Data and Statistics," in UNED–UK, *Gender & Tourism: Women's Employment and Participation in Tourism,* report prepared for the Seventh Session of the UNCSD, April 1999, pp. 17–34; Ida Ayu Agung Mas, "Sua Bali—A Pilot Project on Sustainable Village Tourism in Bali," in UNED–UK, op. cit. this note, pp. 101–112; Regina Scheyvens, "Siyabonga Craft Cooperative: A Case Study," in UNED–UK, op. cit. this note, pp. 149–57.

49. Service jobs from Lee Pera and Deborah McLaren, Rethinking Tourism Project, "Globalization, Tourism & Indigenous Peoples: What You Should Know About the World's Largest 'Industry'," <www.planeta.com/eco travel/resources/rtp/globalization.html>, November 1999; ILO, op. cit. note 42, p. 121; Maggie Black, *In the Twilight Zone: Child Workers in the Hotel,*

Tourism and Catering Industry (Geneva: ILO, 1995); 2 million from ILO, "Seeking Socially Responsible Tourism," *World of Work*, June 2001, pp.10-12.

50. Dependence from Patricia P.A.A.H. Kandelaars, *A Dynamic Simulation Model of Tourism and Environment in the Yucatan Peninsula* (Laxenburg, Austria: International Institute for Applied Systems Analysis, April 1997), p. 2; Sanjay Nepal, "Tourism in Protected Areas: The Nepalese Himalaya," *Annals of Tourism Research*, vol. 27, no. 3 (2000), pp. 661–68; Douglas W. Payne, "Letter from Grenada," *The Nation*, 22 March 1999, pp. 22–24; Tunisia from ILO, "Seeking Socially Responsible Tourism," op. cit. note 49; Frederick Noronha, "Goa's Tourist Boom Backfires With Ugly Smell," *Environment News Service*, 27 December 2000.

51. ILO, *The Social Impact on the Hotel and Tourism Sector of Events Subsequent to 11 September 2001*, briefing paper for discussion at the Informal Meeting on the Hotel and Tourism Sector: Social Impacts of Events Subsequent to 11 September 2001, Geneva, 25–26 October 2001; Club Méditerranée, "Club Méditerranée Announces Measures in Response to the Crisis Provoked by the September 11 Terrorist Attacks," press release (Paris: 19 October 2001).

52. Respect for minorities from Ashley, Boyd, and Goodwin, op. cit. note 10; Bali from Tony Wheeler, "Philosophy of a Guidebook Guru," *UNESCO Courier*, July–August 1999, p. 55; Rachel Proctor, "Tourism Opens New Doors, Creates New Challenges, for Traditional Healers in Peru," *Cultural Survival Quarterly*, winter 2001, pp. 14–16.

53. McLaren, op. cit. note 14, p. 27; Mike Robinson, "Is Cultural Tourism on the Right Track?" *UNESCO Courier*, July–August 1999, pp. 22–23; Menchu quote from Survival, "Tourism and Tribal Peoples: the 'New Imperialism,'" background sheet, <www.survival.org.uk/camp6.htm>, viewed 28 April 1999; Myra Shackley, "The Himalayas: Masked Dances and Mixed Blessings," *UNESCO Courier*, July–August 1999, pp. 28–29.

54. Globalization from Lesley France, ed., *The Earthscan Reader in Sustainable Tourism* (London: Earthscan Publications, Ltd., 1997), p. 8; de Chavez, op. cit. note 32; Peru from Kenneth McCormick, "Can Ecotourism Save the Rainforests?" information sheet (San Francisco: Rainforest Action Network, 1994).

55. John S. Akama, "Marginalization of the Maasai in Kenya," *Annals of Tourism Research*, vol. 26, no. 3 (1996), pp. 716–18; Isaac Sindiga, *Tourism and African Development: Change and Challenge of Tourism in Kenya* (Aldershot, Hamps., U.K. and Leiden, Netherlands: Ashgate Publishing Led and African Studies Centre, 1999), pp. 126–45; benefits from Megan Epler Wood, The International Ecotourism Society (TIES), e-mail to author, 3 October 2001; Tourism Concern, "Burma," <www.tourismconcern.org.uk/campaigns/frame.htm>, viewed 20 September 2001.

56. Robinson, op. cit. note 14, p. 22; Ecuador from Epler Wood, op. cit.

note 55; Stephen G. Snow, "The Kuna General Congress and the Statute on Tourism," *Cultural Survival Quarterly*, winter 2001, pp. 17–18.

57. UNEP, op. cit. note 11; capacity from Pleumarom, op. cit. note 46.

58. Estimate of 90 percent from International Federation Free Trade Union & Trade Union Advisory Committee to the Organisation for Economic Co-operation and Development (OECD), *Tourism and Sustainable Development: Workers and Trade Unions in the Web of Tourism*, Background Paper #2, prepared for the Seventh Session of the UNCSD, New York, 19–30 April 1999, p. 9; most polluting from Milieu Defensie, "The Right Price for Air Travel Campaign," <www.milieudefensie.nl/airtravel/info.htm>, viewed 23 December 1998; shares of transport are 1998 estimates, per WTO, op. cit. note 7, pp. 24–25; 90 percent air travel estimate from World Trade Organization, op. cit. note 7, p. 5.

59. Fastest growing from "Global Warming Could Hurt Tourism," *Associated Press*, 30 August 1999; Intergovernmental Panel on Climate Change (IPCC), *Special Report: Aviation and the Global Atmosphere* (Geneva: 1999); air travel and Figure 4 from Attilio Costaguta, Chief, Statistics & Economic Analysis Section, International Civil Aviation Organization (ICAO), Montreal, e-mail to author, 2 November 1998, and from ICAO, "Strong Airline Passenger Traffic Growth Expected Through 2002," press release (Montreal: 22 June 2000).

60. David Viner and Maureen Agnew, "Climate Change and Its Impacts on Tourism," report prepared for WWF–UK (Norwich, U.K.: University of East Anglia's Climatic Research Unit, July 1999); James J. McCarthy et al., *Climate Change 2001: Impacts, Adaptation, and Vulnerability*, Contribution of Working Group II to the Third Assessment Report of the IPCC (Cambridge, U.K.: Cambridge University Press, 2001), pp. 843–75; 85 percent derived from World Bank, op. cit. note 7, and from WTO, op. cit. note 7, p. 90.

61. UNEP, op. cit. note 11; infrastructure impact from McLaren, op. cit. note 14, p. 30, and from Sven Wunder, *Promoting Forest Conservation through Ecotourism Income?* Occasional Paper No. 21 (Jakarta: Center for International Forestry Research, March 1999); Singy Hanyona, "Victoria Falls Marred by Pollution," *Environment News Service*, 28 September 2000.

62. Larger hotels from WTO, *Tourism Highlights 1999* (Madrid: 19 May 1999), p. 10; room estimates for 1998 and regional breakdown from WTO, op. cit. note 7, p. 29; Caribbean from Pattullo, op. cit. note 44, pp. 107–8.

63. Construction and Cancun from Pattullo, op. cit. note 44, pp. 105–9; "Mexico: Resort's Boom Raises Environmental Concerns," *UN Wire*, 20 August 1999; two ecosystems from Castilho and Herrscher, op. cit. note 45.

64. Estimate of $3.50 from Mitzi Perdue, "Hotels Are Going Green," <www.eggscape.com/hotels.htm>, viewed 9 December 1998; fossil fuel use

from Stefan Gössling, "Tourism—Sustainable Development Option?" *Environmental Conservation*, vol. 27, no. 3 (2000), pp. 223–24.

65. Elisabeth Eaves, "Feature—Dead Sea Tourism Threatens Fragile Environment," *Reuters*, 2 September 1998; Caroline Hawley, "Dead Sea 'to Disappear by 2050,'" *BBC News Online*, 3 August 2001.

66. Golf tourism in Asia from ILO, "Seeking Socially Responsible Tourism," op. cit. note 49; 5,000 hectares and Malaysia from Annette Groth, "Sustainable Tourism and the Environment," *Connect* (UNESCO International Science, Technology & Environmental Education Newsletter), vol. 25, no. 1 (2000), p. 1; water use from Pattullo, op. cit. note 44, p. 107.

67. Diversion and utility prices from UNEP, op. cit. note 11, p. 2; Grenada from Payne, op. cit. note 50, pp. 22–24; WWF International, "Destruction of the Mediterranean by Mass Tourism Poses a Challenge for Industry, Warns WWF," press release (Gland, Switzerland: 1 March 2001); Philippines from Maurice Malanes, "Tourism Killing World's Eighth Wonder," at Third World Network, <www.twnside.org.sg/title/mm-cn.htm>, viewed 18 September 2001.

68. UNEP, op. cit. note 11, p. 2; Noronha, op. cit. note 50.

69. Obstacles to treatment and Caribbean from Pattullo, op. cit. note 44, pp. 112–13; Thailand from James E. N. Sweeting, Aaron G. Bruner, and Amy B. Rosenfeld, *The Green Host Effect*, CI Policy Papers (Washington, DC: Conservation International, 1999), p. 10.

70. Doubling from WTO, op. cit. note 7, p. 59; typical week's output from Kira Schmidt, *Cruising for Trouble: Stemming the Tide of Cruise Ship Pollution* (San Francisco: Bluewater Network, March 2000); 90,000 tons from Honey, op. cit. note 5, p. 40.

71. Douglas Frantz, "Gaps in Sea Laws Shield Pollution by Cruise Lines," *New York Times*, 3 January 1999; "Royal Caribbean Sentenced for Ocean Dumping," *Reuters*, 4 November 1999.

72. New vessels from WTO, op. cit. note 7, p. 59; floating cities from "Cruise Ship Dumping Sparks Interest," *Environmental News Network*, 3 December 1999; passengers and crew from Frantz, op. cit. note 71; eight-story from WTO, "WTO Picks Hot Tourism Trends for 21st Century," press release (Madrid: 4 June 1998); S. H. Smith, "Cruise Ships: A Serious Threat to Coral Reefs and Associated Organisms," *Ocean and Shoreline Management*, vol. 11 (1998), pp. 231–48; Cayman Islands from Pattullo, op. cit. note 44, p. 110.

73. Ill-equipped sites from Paul F. J. Eagles, *International Trends in Park Tourism and Ecotourism* (Waterloo, ON, Canada: University of Waterloo, Department of Recreation and Leisure Studies, 31 August 1999), pp. 28–32;

Machu Picchu from UNESCO, "Information Document: Report of the World Heritage Centre-IUCN-ICOMOS Mission to the Historic Sanctuary of Manchu Picchu, Peru, 18-25 October 1999," prepared for the Twenty-third session of the World Heritage Committee, Marrakesh, Morrocco, 29 November–4 December 1999, p.13; "Cambodia's Tourist Boom Seen Threatening Angkor," *Reuters*, 21 June 2000.

74. "Tourists Soil Malaysia Rain Forest," *Associated Press*, 23 March 1999; safari from Dilys Roe, Nigel Leader-Williams, and Barry Dalal-Clayton, *Take Only Photographs, Leave Only Footprints: The Environmental Impacts of Wildlife Tourism* (London: IIED, October 1997); Costa Rica from McCormick, op. cit. note 54.

75. Jean M. Blane and Reiner Jaakson, "The Impact of Ecotourism Boats on the St Lawrence Beluga Whales," *Environmental Conservation*, autumn 1994, pp. 267–69; Jim Loney, "Bahamas Shark Attack Raises Concerns Over Feeding," *Reuters*, 9 August 2001; safari from Roe, Leader-Williams, and Dalal-Clayton, op. cit. note 74, p. 44; ivory from Danna Harman, "Former Stray Dogs Join Fight to Save Africa's Elephants," *Christian Science Monitor*, 2 July 2001.

76. B. R. Tershy et al, "A Survey of Ecotourism on Islands in Northwestern México," *Environmental Conservation*, vol. 26, no. 3 (1999), pp. 212–17; 66 percent from Samantha Newport, "Oil Spill Highlights Hazards of Isles' Growth," *Washington Post*, 27 January 2001; doubling from Larry Rohter, "Isles Rich in Species Are Origin of Much Tension," *New York Times*, 27 January 2001.

77. UNEP, op. cit. note 11, p. 3; Nepal, op. cit. note 50, pp. 661–81; fuelwood loss from Castilho and Herrscher, op. cit. note 45; Nicodemus Odhiambo, "Millennium Celebrants Swarm to Mt. Kilimanjaro," *Environment News Service*, 20 September 1999.

78. Dive numbers from International Coral Reef Initiative and UNEP, "Tourism and Coral Reefs," information sheet (Nairobi: UNEP, undated); Julie P. Hawkins and Callum M. Roberts, "The Growth of Coastal Tourism in the Red Sea: Present and Future Effects on Coral Reefs," *Ambio*, December 1994, p. 506; Sakanan Plathong, Graeme J. Inglis, and Michael E. Huber, " Effects of Self-Guided Snorkeling Trails on Corals in a Tropical Marine Park," *Conservation Biology*, December 2000, pp. 1821–30; Bonaire from Julie P. Hawkins et al., "Effects of Recreational Scuba Diving on Caribbean Coral and Fish Communities," *Conservation Biology*, August 1999, pp. 888–97; looting from Pattullo, op. cit. note 44, p. 110.

79. Chris Cooper and Stephen Jackson, "Destination Life Cycle: The Isle of Man Case Study," in France, op. cit. note 54, p. 55.

80. Barbados from Pattullo, op. cit. note 44, pp. 106–7; Black Forest and Adriatic from Kandelaars, op. cit. note 50, p. 2; developing world from

Desthuis-Francis, op. cit. note 32, p. 18; Shawn W. Crispin and G. Pierre Goad, "Bangkok Renaissance," *Far Eastern Economic Review*, 30 September 1999, p. 62.

81. TIES, "Ecotourism Statistical Fact Sheet," information sheet (Burlington, VT: 2000); United Nations Economic and Social Council, "Resolution 1998/40 - Declaring the Year 2002 as the International Year of Ecotourism," agreed to at the 46th Plenary Meeting, New York, 30 July 1998.

82. Megan Epler Wood, *Ecotourism: Principles, Practices & Policies for Sustainability* (Nairobi: UNEP and TIES, forthcoming).

83. Honey, op. cit. note 5, p. 5; Cater, op. cit. note 43, p. 88; Peru from Laurent Belsie, "Treading Lightly," *Christian Science Monitor*, 1 February 2001.

84. TIES cited in Mike Tidwell, "No Glaciers in Glacier National Park?" *Washington Post*, 9 September 2001; 7 percent from WTO, op. cit. note 7; 1992 study from Fern Fillion et al., cited in TIES, op. cit. note 81; whale-watching figures include both countries and territories, per Erich Hoyt, *Whale Watching 2000* (Yarmouth Port, MA: International Fund for Animal Welfare, August 2000).

85. Pamela A. White, "North American Ecotourists: Market Profile and Trip Characteristics," *Journal of Travel Research*, spring 1996; survey from Honey, op. cit. note 5, p. 6; Poon, op. cit. note 17, pp. 91–92.

86. Past from Elizabeth Boo, *Ecotourism: The Potentials and Pitfalls, Volume 1* (Washington, DC: World Wildlife Fund, 1990), p. xiv; Caribbean from Nelson Andrade, "Reefs and Reforms," *Our Planet*, vol. 10, no. 1 (1998), p. 18; WTO, op. cit. note 72.

87. Boo, op. cit. note 86, p. xx; Belsie, op. cit. note 83.

88. Increases from Gerard S. Dharmaratne et al., "Tourism Potentials for Financing Protected Areas," *Annals of Tourism Research*, vol. 27, no. 3 (2000), pp. 590–610; South Africa from Eagles, op. cit. note 73, pp. 18–19; Central America from Boo, op. cit. note 86, p. 47.

89. Financing problems from Eagles, op. cit. note 73, pp. 10–18; Dharmaratne et al., op. cit. note 88, pp. 606–7. Box 2 based on the following: Bonaire from John A. Dixon and Tom van't Hof, "Conservation Pays Big Dividends in Caribbean," *Forum for Applied Research and Public Policy*, spring 1997, p. 46; Costa Rica from McCormick, op. cit. note 54; Komodo and Galapagos from Matthew J. Walpole, Harold J. Goodwin, and Kari G. R. Ward, "Pricing Policy for Tourism in Protected Areas: Lessons from Komodo National Park, Indonesia," *Conservation Biology*, February 2001, pp. 223, 219; corruption from Karen Archabald and Lisa Naughton-Treves, "Tourism Revenue-Sharing Around National Parks in Western Uganda: Early Efforts to

Identify and Reward Local Communities," *Environmental Conservation*, vol. 28, no. 2 (2001), pp. 135–49; Mexico from Tershy et al, op. cit. note 76, pp. 212–17; U.S. survey from Castilho and Herrscher, op. cit. note 45; gorillas from Ian Fisher, "Victims of War: The Jungle Gorillas and Tourism," *New York Times*, 31 March 1999; David S. Wilkie and Julia F. Carpenter, "Can Nature Tourism Help Finance Protected Areas in the Congo Basin?" *Oryx*, vol. 33, no. 4 (1999), pp. 332–38.

90. "Freelance Conservationists," *The Economist*, 23 August 2001, p. 62; Costa Rica and Belize from Boo, op. cit. note 86, p. xvii; Jeff Langholz, "Economics, Objectives, and Success of Private Nature Reserves in Sub-Saharan Africa and Latin America," *Conservation Biology*, vol. 10, no. 1 (1996), pp. 271–80.

91. Mark B. Orams, "Towards a More Desirable Form of Ecotourism," *Tourism Management*, vol. 16, no. 1 (1995), p. 3; Marilyn Bauer, "Eco-resort Owner Fights to Save the Ti Ti Monkey," *Environmental News Network*, 21 July 2000.

92. Pleumarom, op. cit. note 46; Ed Stoddard, "Interview-S. Africa Game Parks to Woo Private Sector," *Reuters*, 25 November 1999; John Pomfret, "Privatizing China's Parks," *Washington Post*, 5 July 2001.

93. Pleumarom, op. cit. note 46; Pera and McLaren, op. cit. note 49; Anita Pleumarom, "The Hidden Costs of the 'New' Tourisms—A Focus on Biopiracy," Third World Network Briefing Paper for the Seventh Session of the UNCSD, New York, 1999.

94. Geoffrey Wall, "Is Ecotourism Sustainable?" *Environmental Management*, vol. 2, no. 4 (1997), pp. 9–12; Cater, op. cit. note 43, pp. 86-8; Honey, op. cit. note 5, p. 25.

95. Erlet Cater, "Ecotourism in the Third World—Problems and Prospects for Sustainability," in E. Cater and G. Lowman, *Ecotourism: A Sustainable Option?* (Chichester: Wiley & Sons: 1994), pp. 69–86; Rwanda from Castilho and Herrscher, op. cit. note 45.

96. Fiona Burton, "Can Ecotourism Objectives Be Achieved?" *Annals of Tourism Research*, vol. 25, no. 3 (1998), pp. 755–58; Honey, op. cit. note 5, p. 25; Australia from Chris Ryan, Karen Hughes, and Sharon Chirgwin, "The Gaze, Spectacle and Ecotourism," *Annals of Tourism Research*, vol. 27, no. 1 (2000), pp. 148–63; Cater, op. cit. note 43, p. 88.

97. David B. Weaver, "Magnitude of Ecotourism in Costa Rica and Kenya," *Annals of Tourism Research*, vol. 26, no. 4 (1999), pp. 809–11; "Ecotourism: 'Hordes Of Visitors' Put Costa Rica At Risk," *UN Wire*, 10 May 1999; Amelung et al., op. cit. note 14, p. 95; 700,000 from Costa Rica Tourist Board, "Resume 2000," <www.tourism-costarica.com>, viewed 13 September 2001; Thailand from "Mass (Eco-) Tourism Continues to Ravage Coastal

Areas," *New Frontiers* (Tourism Investigation & Monitoring Team), July–August 1999, pp. 4–5.

98. Keith W. Sproule, "Community-Based Ecotourism Development: Identifying Partners in the Process," in *The Ecotourism Equation: Measuring the Impacts,* Bulletin Series No. 99 (New Haven: Yale University School of Forestry and Environmental Studies, 1996), pp. 233–50; revenue sharing from Archabald and Naughton-Treves, op. cit. note 89, pp. 135-49; infrastructure and overhead from Cater, op. cit. note 95.

99. Rural regions from Cater, op. cit. note 43, p. 85, and from Ashley, Boyd, and Goodwin, op. cit. note 10; Cofan from TIES, "Cultural Impacts," <www.ecotourism.org/travelchoice/cultural.html>, viewed 20 September 2001; Huaorani from Sylvie Blangy, "Ecotourism Without Tears," *UNESCO Courier,* July–August 1999, p. 32.

100. Wunder, op. cit. note 61, pp. 17–19; Archabald and Naughton-Treves, op. cit. note 89, pp. 144–45; quote from Mountain Agenda, "Mountains of the World: Tourism and Sustainable Mountain Development, Part 1," prepared for the Seventh Session of the UNCSD, New York, 19–30 April 1999; CAMPFIRE from Castilho and Herrscher, op. cit. note 45; Nepal from Cater, op. cit. note 95.

101. Wunder, op. cit. note 61, pp. 11–19.

102. Resentment from Cater, op. cit. note 43, p. 88; conflict from Marie Jose Fortin and Christiane Gagnon, "An Assessment of Social Impacts of National Parks on Communities in Quebec, Canada," *Environmental Conservation,* vol. 26, no. 3 (1999), p. 201; Galapagos from Castilho and Herrscher, op. cit. note 45.

103. Partnerships from Sproule, op. cit. note 98, pp. 233–250; 200 guides and 92 percent from Beth Trafk, RARE Center for Tropical Conservation, Arlington, VA, discussion with Uta Saoshiro, Worldwatch Institute, 21 September 2001.

104. Castilho and Herrscher, op. cit. note 45; 1980 numbers from Nepal, op. cit. note 50, p. 669; 63,000 from WWF Nepal, "Conservation and Sustainable Development through Tourism in Nepal," *Ecocircular* (WWF Nepal Program newsletter), March–April 2001, p. 8.

105. Value from Boo, op. cit. note 86, p. xviii; Croatia from "Eco-Tourists Buy Tickets Direct to Conservation," *Environment News Service,* 6 April 2001; The Conference Board, "Business Enterprises for Sustainable Travel's First BEST Practices Highlights Tour Operator's Model Philanthropic Program: Lindblad Guests Have Contributed More than $500,000 to Galapagos Conservation Fund," press release (New York: 12 June 2000).

106. Honey, op. cit. note 5, p. 17; U.S. Agency for International

Development, *Win-Win Approaches to Development and the Environment: Ecotourism and Biodiversity Conservation* (Washington, DC: Center for Development Information and Evaluation, July 1996); Shekhar Singh and Claudio Volonte, *Biodiversity Program Study* (Washington, DC: Global Environment Facility Monitoring and Evaluation Unit, 11 April 2001), pp. 2–3.

107. Sabah from Simon Elegant, "Forest of Contradictions," *Far Eastern Economic Review*, 14 September 2000, pp. 76–79; obstacles from WWF International, "Elephants in the Balance: Conserving Africa's Elephants," <www.panda.org/resources/publications/species/elephants/the_way5.htm>, and from Wunder, op. cit. note 61, p. 17.

108. WTO, "International Year of Ecotourism (IYE) 2002," concept paper (Madrid: undated); Anita Pleumarom, "Do We Need the International Year of Ecotourism?" (Bangkok: Tourism Investigation & Monitoring Team, November 2000).

109. Wall, op. cit. note 94, p. 12; Boo, op. cit. note 86.

110. Definition from WTO, "Concepts & Definitions," <www.world-tourism.org/frameset/frame_sustainable.html>; UN, *Earth Summit Agenda 21: The United Nations Programme of Action from Rio* (New York: 1992); WTTC, WTO, and Earth Council, *Agenda 21 for the Travel & Tourism Industry* (London: 1995); Table 4 based on the following: "Malé Declaration on Tourism & Sustainable Development (1997)," available at <www.eco-tour.org/info/w_10194_en.html>; "Berlin Declaration: Biological Diversity and Sustainable Tourism," available at <www.eco-tour.org/info/w_10016_en.html>; "CSD-7 to Focus on Tourism, Oceans, and SIDS," *CSD Update*, August 1998; action program from Tourism Working Group of the German NGO Forum on Environment and Development, "Position Paper on the Environmental and Social Responsibility of Tourism in the Context of Sustainable Development," November 1998, paper presented to the seventh meeting of the UNCSD, New York, April 1999; "UNEP Principles on the Implementation of Sustainable Tourism," available at <www.unepie.org/pc/tourism/ policy/about_principles.htm>, viewed 21 August 2001; ethics from Cynthia Guttman, "Towards an Ethics of Tourism," *UNESCO Courier*, July–August 1999, p. 56, and from WTO, "Tourism Sector Takes Steps to Ensure Future Growth. Global Code of Ethics Adopted at WTO Summit," press release (Santiago: 1 October 1999); WTO, "WTO and World Bank in New Strategic Alliance," *WTO News*, October–December 1999.

111. Deloitte & Touche, IIED, and ODI, op. cit. note 8; balance from France, op. cit. note 54, p. 23; reconciling perspectives from Stewart Moore and Bill Carter, "Ecotourism in the 21st Century," *Tourism Management*, April 1993, p. 127.

112. U.S. survey cited in TIES, "U.S. Ecotourism Fact Sheet," information

sheet (Burlington, VT: 1999); UK survey from MORI, cited in Green Globe, "Green Globe: Securing the Future for Travel and Tourism," information packet (London: undated).

113. Honey, op. cit. note 5, p. 20; Wolf Michael Iwand, "The Ecological Programme of the TUI," information brochure (Hannover, Germany: Touristic Union International, undated).

114. See International Standards Organization website, <www.iso.org>; UN, op. cit. note 110, p. 237.

115. "Lessening the Environmental Impacts of Leisure Facilities," *Green Hotelier*, April 1999, pp. 18–24; Green Hotels Association, "Ways Hotels are Helping to Save Our Planet," <www.greenhotels.com/grnideas.htm>, viewed 9 December 1998; water savings from Jennifer Bogo, "Breathing Easy in America's First Environmentally-Smart Hotel," *E Magazine*, January/February 2000, p. 47; value and Holiday Inn from Perdue, op. cit. note 64.

116. Rudy Maxa, "Some Savvy Tips on Eco-Travel," *Environmental News Network*, 12 December 1999. Table 5 based on the following sources: International Hotels Environment Initiative (IHEI), "Proving Green Hotel Business is Good Business," information brochure (London: undated); idem, information sheet (London: undated); Bogo, op. cit. note 115, pp. 46–47; Paula Diperna, "Tourism is Only As Sustainable As the Tourism Industry Allows," *Earth Times*, 5 April 1999; Rebecca Hawkins, "Environmental Reviewing for the Hotel Sector: the Experience of Inter-Continental Hotels and Resorts," Tourism Focus No. 5, in *UNEP Industry and Environment*, April–June 1996; Natural Resources Canada, "Canadian Pacific Hotels: Hospitality, Tradition and Good Environmental Stewardship," Energy Efficiency Case Studies (Ottawa: April 1997).

117. IHEI, <www.ihei.org>, viewed 10 October 2001; 111 countries from UN, "Governments, Tour Industry Seek Plan at United Nations to Cut Environmental and Social Impacts," press release (New York: February 1999); UNEP, *Environmental Action Pack for Hotels* (Nairobi: May 1995).

118. Recycling from Mary B. Uebersax, "Indecent Proposal: Cruise Ship Pollution in the Caribbean," August 1996, <www.planeta.com/96/0896cruise.html>, viewed 26 October 2001; newer vessels from "Cruise Line Cleans Up Its Wake," *Environmental News Network*, 6 August 2001, and from "Cruise Companies Aim for Cleaner Waste," *Associated Press*, 31 July 2000; Pattullo, op. cit. note 44, pp. 111–12.

119. International Council of Cruise Lines, "ICCL Industry Standard E-01-01: Cruise Industry Waste Management Practices and Procedures," adopted 11 June 2001, available at <www.iccl.org/policies/environmental standards.pdf>.

120. Guide programs from Thomas B. Lawrence and Deborah Wickins, "Managing Legitimacy in Ecotourism," *Tourism Management*, vol. 18, no. 5 (1997), p. 313.

121. UNEP, "UNEP, WTO and Tour Operators Join Forces to Promote Sustainable Tourism Development," press release (Nairobi: 19 April 1999); members from <www.toinitiative.org/initiative.htm>, viewed 17 September 2001; Jan Jackson, "The Environmental Programme of British Airways Holidays," Tourism Focus No. 7, in *UNEP Industry and Environment*, October–December 1996.

122. Australia from R. C. Buckley and G. F. Araujo, "Environmental Management Performance in Tourism Accommodation," *Annals of Tourism Research*, vol. 24, no. 2 (1997), pp. 465–70; UNEP, op. cit. note 11, pp. 5–6, 10

123. UNEP, op. cit. note 11, pp. 5–6, 10; monitoring from Cater, op. cit. note 43, p. 90.

124. UNEP, *Environmental Codes of Conduct for Tourism* (Nairobi: 1995); International Association of Antarctic Tour Operators website, <www.iaato.org >, viewed 10 October 2001; "Antarctic Tourism Tests Fragile Ecosystem," *Reuters*, 23 February 1999.

125. UNEP, *Ecolabels in the Tourism Industry* (Nairobi: October 1998); Tanja Mihali, "Ecological Labelling in Tourism," in Lino Briguglio et al., eds. *Sustainable Tourism in Island & Small States: Issues and Policies* (London: Pinter, 1996), pp. 197–205; Ron Mader, "Eco-yardsticks for Hotels—Whose to Use?" *EcoAmericas*, December 1999, p. 8. Table 6 based on the following: Green Globe 21 from UN, op. cit. note 117, from Green Globe website, <www.greenglobe21.org>, and from Synergy, "Tourism Certification: An Analysis of Green Globe 21 and Other Tourism Certification Programs," report prepared for WWF International (Gland, Switzerland: August 2000); Ecotel from <www.ecotels.org>, viewed 10 September 2001; Blue Flag from <www.blueflag.org> and from Graham Ashworth, "The Blue Flag Campaign," *Naturopa* no. 88, (1998), p. 21; Certification for Sustainable Tourism from <www.turismo-sostenible.co.cr>, viewed 10 October 2001, from Diane Jukofsky, "Costa Rica Rates Hotels for Eco-Friendliness," *Environment News Service*, 14 December 1999, and from Beatrice Blake, "Comparing the ICT's Certification of Sustainable Tourism and the New Key to Costa Rica's Sustainable Tourism Rating," August 2001, <www.planeta.com/planeta/01/0104costa.html>, viewed 7 September 2001; Rainforest Alliance, "About SmartVoyager," <www.rainforest-alliance. org/programs/sv/index.html>, viewed 21 August 2001; Jorge Peraza-Breedy, Sustainable Tourism Program, Rainforest Alliance, San José, Costa Rica, e-mail to author, 21 August 2001; Green Leaf Foundation, "Profile: Green Leaf Program," informational brochure (Bangkok: undated); number of hotels with Green Leaf from UNEP, Regional Office for Asia and the Pacific, "Thailand's Green Tourism Initiative Applauded," press release (Bangkok: 2 October 2000).

126. Synergy, op. cit. note 125; Anne Becher and Beatrice Blake, "Reflections on 'Green' Ratings," *La Planeta Platica*, August 1998.

127. Honey, op. cit. note 5, p. 32; Pleumarom, op. cit. note 46.

128. UNED–UK, op. cit. note 28, p. 5; "Recruiting From and Training the Local Community," *Green Hotelier*, April 1999, pp. 12–13; Paula Szuchman, "Profit and Progress," *Condé Nast Traveler*, July 2000, p. 58; Business Enterprises for Sustainable Travel, "Making Tourism Work for Africa's Developing Economies," *BEST Practices* (New York: 2001)

129. Cater, op. cit. note 95, pp. 69–86; Honey, op. cit. note 5, p. 87; Alan Flook, "The Changing Structure of International Trade in Tourism Services, The Tour Operators Perspective," presentation at WTO Symposium on Tourism Services, Geneva, 22–23 February 2001, p. 7.

130. UNCTAD, op. cit. note 6, pp. 16–17; Barbara Jones and Tanya Tear, "Australia's National Ecotourism Strategy," Tourism Focus No. 1, in *UNEP Industry and Environment*, January–March 1995; Gunnar Zettersten, "Recommendation on Sustainable Tourism," *Naturopa* no. 88 (1998), p. 15.

131. Trish Nicholson, *Culture, Tourism and Local Strategies Towards Development: Case Studies in the Philippines and Vietnam*, ESCOR Research Report #R6578 (London: UKDFID, 1997).

132. Sproule, op. cit. note 98; Brian Wheeller, "Tourism's Troubled Times: Responsible Tourism is Not the Answer," in France, op. cit. note 54, pp. 63–4; Wunder, op. cit. note 61, pp. 11–17; Cater, op. cit. note 95; Deloitte & Touche, IIED, and ODI, op. cit. note 8.

133. Walpole and Goodwin, op. cit. note 41, p. 573; Wheeller, op. cit. note 132, p. 63–4; Wunder, op. cit. note 61, pp. 11–17; Deloitte & Touche, IIED, and ODI, op. cit. note 8; Sproule, op. cit. note 98; WWF Nepal, op. cit. note 104.

134. Licensing and training from Sproule, op. cit. note 98; UNCTAD, op. cit. note 6, p. 15; Honey, op. cit. note 5, p. 83; Deloitte & Touche, IIED, and ODI, op. cit. note 8; "Tourism in South Africa: Image Problem," *The Economist*, 16 December 2000, p. 69.

135. Ashley, Boyd, and Goodwin, op. cit. note 10; Walpole and Goodwin, op. cit. note 41, p. 573; Deloitte & Touche, IIED, and ODI, op. cit. note 8; Sustainable Travel & Tourism, "Nepal Bans Child Labour in Tourism," *News*, June 2001, <www.sustravel.com>.

136. Diverse needs from E. Cater and B. Goodall, "Must Tourism Destroy Its Resource Base?," in France, op. cit. note 54, p. 86; Julio Batle, "Rethinking Tourism in the Balearic Islands," *Annals of Tourism Research*, vol. 27, no. 2 (2000), pp. 524–26; Egypt et al. from UNEP, op. cit. note 11, p. 7; Nicole Winfield, "Cuba Seeks Right Mix of Eco-tourism," <msnbc.com>, 20 November 2000.

137. Saren Starbridge and Peter Bramwell, "Charging for Rhinos: Making Conservation Pay," *Living Planet*, spring 2001, pp. 64–69; Wouter Schalken, "Where are the Wild Ones? The Involvement of Indigenous Communities in Tourism in Namibia," *Cultural Survival Quarterly*, summer 1999, pp. 40–42; Namibia Community Based Tourism Association, <www.nacobta.com.na>, viewed 19 September 2001.

138. John Roach, "Peru Puts Limits on Inca Trail Foot Traffic," *Environmental News Network*, 18 May 2000; Kingdom of Bhutan, <www.kingdomof bhutan.com>, viewed 11 July 2001; Mridula Chettri, "High Altitude Dilemma," *Down to Earth*, 30 September 2000, p. 30; Ecuador from Castilho and Herrscher, op. cit. note 45.

139. Deepak Gajurel, "Plastic Bags Banned from Nepal's Trekking Regions," *Environment News Service*, 6 October 2000; Ministry of Tourism, Government of Nepal, "Minimum Impact Code for Travel to Upper Mustang" (Kathmandu: 2000).

140. Sweeting et al., op. cit. note 69, pp. 64–69; France from UNEP, op. cit. note 11, p. 4; "London Air Travellers Asked to Pay for Polluting Planes," *Reuters*, 29 June 2001.

141. "Spain's Balearics Approve Tourist Eco-tax," *Reuters*, 12 April 2001; Chris Brown, "Spain Blames Strikes, Eco-Tax for Tourism Slowdown," *Reuters*, 1 August 2001; Seychelles from UNEP, op. cit. note 11, p. 4, and from Seychelles New Adventures, "Passport, Visa, and Customs," <www.sey.net/trv_pp.htm>, viewed 10 October 2001; cruise tax and tax holidays from Cater, op. cit. note 95.

142. Chee Yoke Ling, "Tourism and Biodiversity: 'No' to Global Guidelines," *New Frontiers* (Tourism Investigation & Monitoring Team), September–October 1998.

143. Ashley, Boyd, and Goodwin, op. cit. note 10; Asian Development Bank, "Helping Cook Islands Manage Waste Will Reduce Health Risks, Protect Environment," press release (Manila: 17 July 2001).

144. WTO, "WTO and the Environment," press release (Madrid: 27 April 1995); International Maritime Organization website, <www.imo.org>.

145. Lawrence and Wickins, op. cit. note 120, p. 315; best practices from UNEP Division of Technology, Industry and Economics website, <www.uneptie.org/pc/tourism/home.htm>.

146. Maria Kousis, "Tourism and the Environment: A Social Movements Perspective," *Annals of Tourism Research* vol. 27, no. 2 (2000), pp. 468–89; Robyn Bushell, Head, Tourism Academic Group, University of Western Sydney, Australia, e-mail to author, 6 October 2001.

147. Chelaton, op. cit. note 1.

148. Wendy Patterson, "Mexican Government Temporarily Revokes License Granted to Build Along Coastal Area," *International Environment Reporter*, 25 April 2001, pp. 322–23; 40 species from "Corporate Corner," *EarthNet News*, 1 July 1999; Tourism Concern, "Burma," op. cit. note 55.

149. United Nations, "UN Talks With Tourism Industry Spur Plans to Cut Negative Impacts," press release (New York: 3 May 1999); Tourism Concern, "Child Sex Tourism," <www.tourismconcern.org.uk/useful%20stuff/frame.htm>, viewed 20 September 2001; WTTC from Cynthia Guttman, "Towards an Ethics of Tourism," *UNESCO Courier*, July–August 1999, p. 56.

150. TIES, "'Your Travel Choice Makes a Difference' Campaign," press release (Burlington, VT: 29 February 2000); see also <www.ecotourism.org/travelchoice/index.htm>; Conservation International's Ecotravel Center, at <www.ecotour.org>; see <www.responsibletravel.com>.

151. TIES, "Cultural Impacts," op. cit. note 99.

Worldwatch Papers

No. of Copies

_____WWP0159 Traveling Light: New Paths for International Tourism

Climate Change, Energy, and Materials

_____WWP0157 Hydrogen Futures: Toward a Sustainable Energy System
_____WWP0151 Micropower: The Next Electrical Era
_____WWP0149 Paper Cuts: Recovering the Paper Landscape
_____WWP0144 Mind Over Matter: Recasting the Role of Materials in Our Lives
_____WWP0138 Rising Sun, Gathering Winds: Policies to Stabilize the Climate and Strengthen Economies
_____WWP0130 Climate of Hope: New Strategies for Stabilizing the World's Atmosphere
_____WWP0124 A Building Revolution: How Ecology and Health Concerns Are Transforming Construction

Ecological and Human Health

_____WWP0158 Unnatural Disasters
_____WWP0153 Why Poison Ourselves? A Precautionary Approach to Synthetic Chemicals
_____WWP0148 Nature's Cornucopia: Our Stake in Plant Diversity
_____WWP0145 Safeguarding The Health of Oceans
_____WWP0142 Rocking the Boat: Conserving Fisheries and Protecting Jobs
_____WWP0141 Losing Strands in the Web of Life: Vertebrate Declines and the Conservation of Biological Diversity
_____WWP0140 Taking a Stand: Cultivating a New Relationship with the World's Forests
_____WWP0129 Infecting Ourselves: How Environmental and Social Disruptions Trigger Disease
_____WWP0128 Imperiled Waters, Impoverished Future: The Decline of Freshwater Ecosystems

Economics, Institutions, and Security

_____WWP0155 Still Waiting for the Jubilee: Pragmatic Solutions for the Third World Debt Crisis
_____WWP0152 Working for the Environment: A Growing Source of Jobs
_____WWP0146 Ending Violent Conflict
_____WWP0139 Investing in the Future: Harnessing Private Capital Flows for Environmentally Sustainable Development
_____WWP0137 Small Arms, Big Impact: The Next Challenge of Disarmament
_____WWP0134 Getting the Signals Right: Tax Reform to Protect the Environment and the Economy
_____WWP0133 Paying the Piper: Subsidies, Politics, and the Environment
_____WWP0127 Eco-Justice: Linking Human Rights and the Environment
_____WWP0126 Partnership for the Planet: An Environmental Agenda for the United Nations
_____WWP0125 The Hour of Departure: Forces That Create Refugees and Migrants

Food, Water, Population, and Urbanization

_____WWP0156 City Limits: Putting the Brakes on Sprawl
_____WWP0150 Underfed and Overfed: The Global Epidemic of Malnutrition
_____WWP0147 Reinventing Cities for People and the Planet
_____WWP0143 Beyond Malthus: Sixteen Dimensions of the Population Problem
_____WWP0136 The Agricultural Link: How Environmental Deterioration Could Disrupt Economic Progress
_____WWP0135 Recycling Organic Waste: From Urban Pollutant to Farm Resource
_____WWP0132 Dividing the Waters: Food Security, Ecosystem Health, and the New Politics of Scarcity
_____WWP0131 Shrinking Fields: Cropland Loss in a World of Eight Billion

_____Total copies (transfer number to order form on next page)

PUBLICATION ORDER FORM

NOTE: Many Worldwatch publications can be downloaded as PDF files from our website at **www.worldwatch.org**. Orders for printed publications can also be placed on the web.

_____ *State of the World:* **$15.95**
The annual book used by journalists, activists, scholars, and policymakers worldwide to get a clear picture of the environmental problems we face.

_____ **State of the World Library: $39.00 (international subscribers $49)**
Receive *State of the World* and all Worldwatch Papers as they are released during the calendar year.

_____ *Vital Signs:* **$13.95**
The book of trends that are shaping our future in easy-to-read graph and table format, with a brief commentary on each trend.

_____ WORLD WATCH **magazine subscription: $25.00 (international subscribers $40.00)**
Stay abreast of global environmental trends and issues with our award-winning, eminently readable bimonthly magazine.

_____ **Worldwatch CD-ROM: $99.00**
Contains global agricultural, energy, economic, environmental, social, and military indicators from all current Worldwatch publications. Includes *Vital Signs* and *State of the World* as they are published. CD contains Microsoft Excel spreadsheets 5.0/95 (*.xls) for Windows, and works on both Mac and PC.

_____ **Worldwatch Papers—See list on previous page Single copy: $5.00**
any combination of titles: 2–5: $4.00 ea. • 6–20: $3.00 ea. • 21 or more: $2.00 ea.

$4.00* Shipping and Handling *($8.00 outside North America)*
   minimum charge for S&H; call (888) 544-2303 for bulk order S&H
_____ **TOTAL** (U.S. dollars only)

Make check payable to: Worldwatch Institute, P.O. Box 188, Williamsport, PA 17703-9913

❑ Enclosed is my check or purchase order for U.S. $_____

❑ AMEX ❑ VISA ❑ MasterCard _____
                             Card Number   Expiration Date

signature

name   **daytime phone #**

address

city   **state**   **zip/country**

phone: (888) 544-2303 or (570) 320-2076   fax: (570) 320-2079
e-mail: wwpub@worldwatch.org   website: www.worldwatch.org

Wish to make a tax-deductible contribution? Contact Worldwatch to find out how your donation can help advance our work.

Worldwatch Papers

No. of Copies

_____WWP0159 Traveling Light: New Paths for International Tourism

Climate Change, Energy, and Materials

_____WWP0157 Hydrogen Futures: Toward a Sustainable Energy System
_____WWP0151 Micropower: The Next Electrical Era
_____WWP0149 Paper Cuts: Recovering the Paper Landscape
_____WWP0144 Mind Over Matter: Recasting the Role of Materials in Our Lives
_____WWP0138 Rising Sun, Gathering Winds: Policies to Stabilize the Climate and Strengthen Economies
_____WWP0130 Climate of Hope: New Strategies for Stabilizing the World's Atmosphere
_____WWP0124 A Building Revolution: How Ecology and Health Concerns Are Transforming Construction

Ecological and Human Health

_____WWP0158 Unnatural Disasters
_____WWP0153 Why Poison Ourselves? A Precautionary Approach to Synthetic Chemicals
_____WWP0148 Nature's Cornucopia: Our Stake in Plant Diversity
_____WWP0145 Safeguarding The Health of Oceans
_____WWP0142 Rocking the Boat: Conserving Fisheries and Protecting Jobs
_____WWP0141 Losing Strands in the Web of Life: Vertebrate Declines and the Conservation of Biological Diversity
_____WWP0140 Taking a Stand: Cultivating a New Relationship with the World's Forests
_____WWP0129 Infecting Ourselves: How Environmental and Social Disruptions Trigger Disease
_____WWP0128 Imperiled Waters, Impoverished Future: The Decline of Freshwater Ecosystems

Economics, Institutions, and Security

_____WWP0155 Still Waiting for the Jubilee: Pragmatic Solutions for the Third World Debt Crisis
_____WWP0152 Working for the Environment: A Growing Source of Jobs
_____WWP0146 Ending Violent Conflict
_____WWP0139 Investing in the Future: Harnessing Private Capital Flows for Environmentally Sustainable Development
_____WWP0137 Small Arms, Big Impact: The Next Challenge of Disarmament
_____WWP0134 Getting the Signals Right: Tax Reform to Protect the Environment and the Economy
_____WWP0133 Paying the Piper: Subsidies, Politics, and the Environment
_____WWP0127 Eco-Justice: Linking Human Rights and the Environment
_____WWP0126 Partnership for the Planet: An Environmental Agenda for the United Nations
_____WWP0125 The Hour of Departure: Forces That Create Refugees and Migrants

Food, Water, Population, and Urbanization

_____WWP0156 City Limits: Putting the Brakes on Sprawl
_____WWP0150 Underfed and Overfed: The Global Epidemic of Malnutrition
_____WWP0147 Reinventing Cities for People and the Planet
_____WWP0143 Beyond Malthus: Sixteen Dimensions of the Population Problem
_____WWP0136 The Agricultural Link: How Environmental Deterioration Could Disrupt Economic Progress
_____WWP0135 Recycling Organic Waste: From Urban Pollutant to Farm Resource
_____WWP0132 Dividing the Waters: Food Security, Ecosystem Health, and the New Politics of Scarcity
_____WWP0131 Shrinking Fields: Cropland Loss in a World of Eight Billion

_____Total copies (transfer number to order form on next page)

PUBLICATION ORDER FORM

NOTE: Many Worldwatch publications can be downloaded as PDF files from our website at **www.worldwatch.org**. Orders for printed publications can also be placed on the web.

_____ *State of the World:* **$15.95**
The annual book used by journalists, activists, scholars, and policymakers worldwide to get a clear picture of the environmental problems we face.

_____ **State of the World Library: $39.00 (international subscribers $49)**
Receive *State of the World* and all Worldwatch Papers as they are released during the calendar year.

_____ *Vital Signs:* **$13.95**
The book of trends that are shaping our future in easy-to-read graph and table format, with a brief commentary on each trend.

_____ **WORLD WATCH magazine subscription: $25.00 (international subscribers $40.00)**
Stay abreast of global environmental trends and issues with our award-winning, eminently readable bimonthly magazine.

_____ **Worldwatch CD-ROM: $99.00**
Contains global agricultural, energy, economic, environmental, social, and military indicators from all current Worldwatch publications. Includes *Vital Signs* and *State of the World* as they are published. CD contains Microsoft Excel spreadsheets 5.0/95 (*.xls) for Windows, and works on both Mac and PC.

_____ **Worldwatch Papers—See list on previous page Single copy: $5.00**
any combination of titles: 2–5: $4.00 ea. • 6–20: $3.00 ea. • 21 or more: $2.00 ea.

$4.00* Shipping and Handling *($8.00 outside North America)*
   minimum charge for S&H; call (888) 544-2303 for bulk order S&H

_____ **TOTAL** (U.S. **dollars only)**

Make check payable to: Worldwatch Institute, P.O. Box 188, Williamsport, PA 17703-9913

❑ Enclosed is my check or purchase order for U.S. $_____

❑ AMEX ❑ VISA ❑ MasterCard _____
                                    Card Number   Expiration Date

_____
signature

_____
name   **daytime phone #**

_____
address

_____
city   **state**   **zip/country**

phone: (888) 544-2303 or (570) 320-2076   fax: (570) 320-2079
e-mail: wwpub@worldwatch.org   website: www.worldwatch.org

Wish to make a tax-deductible contribution? Contact Worldwatch to find out how your donation can help advance our work.